101 Habits for Highly Successful Living

By Greg Parry PhD

IMPORTANT INFORMATION

The information provided in this book is designed to provide helpful information on the subjects discussed. This book is not meant to be used, nor should it be used, to diagnose or treat any medical condition. For diagnosis or treatment of any medical problem, consult your own physician. The publisher and author are not responsible for any specific health or allergy needs that may require medical supervision and are not liable for any damages or negative consequences from any treatment, action, application or preparation, to any person reading or following the information in this book. References are provided for informational purposes only and do not constitute endorsement of any websites or other sources. Readers should be aware that the websites listed in this book may change.

Copyright © 2014 by Beran Parry

All rights reserved. No part of this publication may be reproduced, distributed, or transmitted in any form or by any means, including photocopying, recording, or other electronic or mechanical methods, without the prior written permission of the publisher, except in the case of brief quotations embodied in critical reviews and certain other non-commercial uses permitted by copyright law. For permission requests, write to the author's email address: beranparry@gmail.com

Acknowledgement

Writing can be a particularly challenging experience but the project was supported and encouraged by a bold and brave crew of enthusiasts who generously lent their time, expertise and creativity to the book and I'm grateful to each and every one of them.

My wife, Beran, who has worked tirelessly to prepare my book and has headed up and directed the support team, ably assisted by my talented colleague, Kevin Wallington.

SPECIAL FREE GIFT FOR YOU

.....enjoy this free ebook

Go to the free book page on this website...

http://www.onelifeblog.com

SPECIAL FREE GIFT FOR YOU

.....enjoy this free ebook

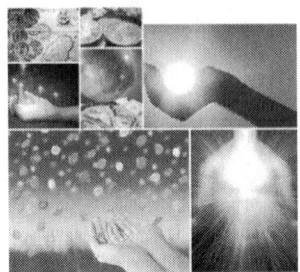

http://www.onelifeblog.com

About the Author

Initially I trained in the field of Corporate Psychology and Management, gaining a PhD along the way and spending most of my time driving commercial projects and delivering Motivational Training in a corporate environment. And there were catalysts for change that appeared quite unexpectedly. I've been privileged to sit at the feet of some quite extraordinary financial giants, individuals who carved out their success from the bare rock of their own determination and dogged persistence. These were highly motivated and inspiring people and it's largely thanks to their advice and unwavering examples that I've been able to create a lifestyle that allows me to enjoy the kind of freedom that most people only dream about.

MY INSPIRATION

I have been extremely fortunate to work with a surprising number of self-made billionaires, individuals who were generous enough to share their experiences and their personal philosophy of success with me. Some of them were kind enough to mentor me during my earlier years and this generosity has prompted me to publish and share some of the jewels of their accumulated wisdom and add weight to the argument that success is not an accident.

As well as studying the architecture of material success, these individuals also dwelt on the importance of creating balance in life, of creating time to be with their families, to support great causes and to make a difference to the quality of peoples' lives. They appreciated the freedom that their lifestyles had created for themselves and displayed a breath-taking lack of selfishness in promoting success wherever they found fertile ground in which their advice could take root. One of them described this spirit of generosity as a personal legacy, a way of ensuring that all of his hard-won lessons were not simply confined to the limits of his own life.

There's a great deal of material in the marketplace today on the subject of success. Against this dense background of conflicting ideas and approaches, perhaps we should determine from the outset what success really entails.

I subscribe to my mentors' philosophy of personal freedom, of creating sufficient wealth to live the way you want to live and to enjoy the gift of this life to the full. You'll feel a lot better when you share your success with others too. You certainly don't have to be a billionaire to achieve that level of freedom and personal choice or to make a difference to the lives of others. But you do need the appropriate attitude. You will need determination and you'll probably need to make some adjustments to how you think, feel and behave. Letting go of old habits, shaking yourself loose from the grip of the past, learning to focus on a much brighter vision of the future – these are all components that will enhance your chances for success and improve the quality of your daily life at every level. It isn't simply a question of how much cash you've stashed away. The picture's bigger, more detailed, more encompassing and brighter than you might've thought possible. Success is certainly about measurable achievement but it also involves a stronger connections to the people around us. It involves a deep sense of peace within ourselves. It encapsulates the concept of personal acceptance. It permits us to choose appropriate goals and to follow the winding pathway to our destination with unbreakable confidence in our ability to get wherever we choose to go. And, if the seeds of wisdom have taken root, to enjoy the journey to the full.

Table of Contents

Acknowledgement

About the Author

Foreword

Introduction

1. Purpose. Understanding why you're here and what you want from the experience

2. Peace and calm. Loosening the lifelong bonds of stress.

3. Real energy. Feeling the Force of your natural energy source

4. Dreams. Accessing the profound insights and analysis of the subconscious super-computer

5. Fuel. Respecting your body's need for the most natural nutrition

6. Positive Influences and the hidden power of our expectations.

7. Rest 'n' Recovery. New habits to promote great sleep

8. Stretch It. A supple body support a flexible mind

9. Creativity. Unleash the power of your Hidden Muse

10 Identity. Revealing the deeper sense of Self

11. Nature. Re-connecting with the natural environment

12. Parents. Making peace with the first relationships and building a foundation for the future

13. Work. Finding the perfect way to express who you really are

14. Chill. Unlocking the physical armour of your daily stress and learn to feel free

15. Awareness. Taking control of the inner realms of our thoughts and feelings

16. Getting down to the details. Building your personal priority List

17. Sleep. Maximising your daily down time to improve brain function

18. Move. Appreciating the miracle of your body

19. Flexibility. Keep your joints in great working order and move more easily

20. Your Word. Empowering the value of what you say

21. Change. The irresistible power of choice

22. Feelings. Taming our emotional habits

23. Focus. Choosing to connect with positive outcomes

24. Goals. Keeping your attention on your chosen destination

25. Visualise. Use your imagination to lift your spirits

26. Determination. Persistence paves the way to success and fulfilment

27. Appreciation and the Art of Being Grateful

28. Generosity. Celebrate success wherever you find it

29. Cash. Learning to be completely at ease with the power of money

30. Will and the extraordinary focus of a trained and flexible mind

31. Freedom. The fuller expression of total success

32. Habits. Moving the framework of perception to change the universe

33. Hydrate. The magical power of H2O

34. Happiness as a way of experiencing the world

35. Awaken. Developing the power of perception

36. Negativity. Releasing yourself from the lifelong habit of negative feelings

37. Action. Seize the moment. Seize the day

38. Influence. Touching the lives of everyone you meet

39. Choose. Becoming the origin of everything you feel

40. Judgement. Banishing the veil of delusion that clouds our perception

41. Tuning in and tuning out

FREE GIFT FOR YOU OUR READER

42. Identity. The power of being who you really are

43. Control flows so easily from your posture

44. Obstructions. Obstacles or excuses?

45. Problems. The ability to place difficulties into their wider perspective

46. Letting go of the past and discovering a brilliantly illuminated future

47. The Core. Making the most of your inner strength

48. Stripping away the illusion of protective armour

49. Isolation. Being totally present with other people

50. Acceptance. The power of being you

51. Laughter. The ultimate weapon to wield against the illusion of fear

52. Perspective.

53. Power and the absolute intensity of the trained Will

54. Habits and the Way of Total Health

55. Get creative.

56. Sleep and the art of passive refreshment

57. Words and the language of powerful intent

58. Greatness is the natural human condition

59. Acceptance and gratitude for the miracle of your body

60. Liberation and the magnificence of letting go

62. Blame and the failure to take full responsibility

63. Harness the Force of the Focused Mind

64. Fixing yourself by giving permission to get better

65. Cosmos and the appreciation of the Infinite

66. Take another shot at your personal Hit List.

67. You and the need for private space

68. Belief and the irresistible drive of your vision

69. Balance and the art of making time for the important things in your life

70. Laughter is just so wonderfully good for you.

71. Vocabulary and the power of our words

72. Inspiration.

73. Compromise and the obvious evidence of a truly successful life

74. Enough effort can move a mountain

75. The world you create is largely in your head.

76. Victory and the reassuring log of your achievements and successes

77. Inner joy and the pathway to internal calm, serenity and abiding peace

78. Challenging the familiar mental landscape

79. Stand up and relieve the tension in your muscles and joints

80. Sweet, white and deadly. The danger of sugar

81. The evil weed. Time to quit and place your vote for health and wellbeing

82. Go natural. Choose the best fuel for your mind and for your body

83. Grin and learn to enjoy your success every day

84. Are you happy with your own company?

85. Suspend all critical and destructive judgement of your body

86. Take a load off your feet and off your stomach

87. Whining and demeaning

88. Posture Checking. Attitude adjusting.

89. Adequate Vitamin D. Get some rays!

90. Amore and the building blocks of the Universe

91. Data overload and the space within ourselves.

92. The eternal power of the present moment

93. Being real. Being who you are

94. Harnessing the power of change.

95. Emotional energy and the powerhouse that drives the Universe

96. Recognising the power and value of our dreams

97. You are what you think.

98. Once you accept the power of choice in your life, everything begins to move forwards

99. Reviewing progress and taking the next step.

100. Drink deeply from the wellspring of your deeper mind.

101. The imagination. Visualising the brightest possible future

FREE GIFT FOR YOU OUR READER

Other books Edited by Greg Parry

Foreword

Life is about change. Everything around us is constantly changing, from the vibrations in the molecules that make up our bodies to the swirling dance and movement of galactic clusters. Everything is moving and everything is changing. It's the natural order of the universe. Change is the force that opens up opportunities with every new breath.

Yet we humans resist change at every level of our consciousness. We become locked into our old habits, thinking the same thoughts, feeling the same feelings, clinging to the familiar ways of experiencing life regardless of the outcomes. Our objective is to help you to embrace change and make it work for you. Our mission is to show you that life really can be better. Not by staying in the old patterns of stress and limitation but by introducing subtle shifts in behaviour that can expand awareness and put you firmly in control of a process that can revolutionise your life. Change is normal, natural and inevitable. So let's harness its potential and start living life to the full. The world is full of fabulous and inspiring examples of extraordinary individuals who have broken free of their conditioning and apparent limitations and created success at every level of their lives. The good news is that you're going to be making the rules. You're going to be in control. It's your life. It's only right that you should choose how it works out.

Introduction

Welcome to your new future.

Welcome to your **101 Habits of Truly Successful Living**

We're starting from the basic premise that there are some areas of your life that probably need help. Well that's no great surprise. You're human. It's part of the package of being a member of the great clan we know today as Homo Sapiens. Welcome to the human condition!

Some of the methods described in your **101 Habits of Truly Successful Living** will focus specifically on how you use your mind and body and will help you to master a range of important, practical, physical and mental skills. There are distinct physical connections between how you use your body and the way you think and feel.

Our aim is to teach you how to overcome some of the shortcomings that often get in the way of your full potential. Other methods have been harnessed to target and address the mental, emotional and psychological components that contribute towards living life to the full.

Clearly, before we get started, the first question we need to ask is "Are you really happy?" Have you even stopped for a moment and asked yourself that question recently? It's a very important issue.

If you have to think about it, the answer is probably "No"! You know if you're really happy and I'm not referring to some superficial, transient approximation of happiness. I'm talking about a fundamental force within us all that is so powerful that it can sustain us like a miniature sun shining in our hearts. Life is too precious to be wasted on unhappiness. If you suspect that there can be more to your life, this is your chance to discover and deploy that latent potential.

We want you to feel great, to find an outlet for your talents, to feel that you have purpose, to take control of your life, to reap the rewards of your success. The good news is that no one else is going to do it for you. The power and the responsibility are completely in your own hands, my friend. The 101 Habits are designed to help you maximise your potential and to enjoy life to the full. Many of these ideas have been synthesised from countless meetings and conversations with extremely successful individuals, people who went far beyond the theoretical stage and put the ideas powerfully and tenaciously into practice. Some of the techniques have an ancient lineage, often drawn from the traditions of civilisations that spent centuries exploring the underlying nature of the human condition.

As a species, we haven't changed very much in millennia so the insights and conclusions are as useful for us today as they were for our distant ancestors all those thousands of years ago. Other methods are also drawn from the very latest and often surprising research into human brain function. Whatever the source, we're bringing methods to you that work!

I want you to accept right now that you are the power source. You are the engine. Your actions will determine the outcome. This is not Harry Potter. This is the beautiful, real world where great things happen because great people - just like you - do the essential things that make a real difference to their lives. And that's when truly amazing things happen.

So buckle up and enjoy the ride. The journey is about to begin!

1. Purpose. Understanding why you're here and what you want from the experience

Do you know your purpose? One of the most helpful and perhaps most powerful dynamics in our lives is having a really clear and well-defined sense of purpose. People with purpose don't let obstacles get in their way. If you don't have a purpose, it's far too easy to drift through life without really knowing what you're here for. So I'd like you to pause for a moment and ask yourself if you really know what you want.

Don't rush and don't be surprised if the answer is 'No'. Most people don't really know what they want beyond the demands and challenges of their daily existence. So your first task on this first day of revolutionising your life is to take a moment to reflect more deeply and see if you can work out what you really want. It's your life here and I'm asking you to choose something worthwhile. It can be one of the most revealing exercises in your earthly existence. It can power you up and become your personal, daily source of inspiration. Take a piece of paper and a pen and write down your conclusions.

Write down a list of whatever you want. The list can include absolutely anything: material goods, wealth, better health, peace, great relationships. It's your list. You write down whatever comes to mind. It's a private list. It is not for sharing nor is it intended for discussion.

When you've finished, put the list somewhere safe and let it lie for a few days. Look at your ideas again in two or three days time. Review your list and see if your ideas, plans and goals look different. Feel free to alter, delete or amend anything. It's your list. Which items really grab your attention? Which items give you an emotional buzz? Those are the items to start with. Now that you know which items are the most important, you need do something, anything, to make them a reality. Take some time to think about how you could achieve your goal. Get a little wild in your thinking. Get creative. Do some research. See what needs to be done to get you started.

Find your purpose. Then move towards it. Right now. The first step is always the most important.

2. Peace and calm. Loosening the lifelong bonds of stress.

Not a hippy mantra but a powerful insight into human creativity. Stress is a habit. An addictive behaviour that blights our lives and diminishes our natural creativity. Cultivating calm in our lives is a hidden and powerful secret that really increases and enhances our latent creativity. Calm helps us to focus on our tasks without the usual intrusions of tension or stress. Most of your stress is completely unnecessary and an obstacle to real progress. Stress is after all just a habit, a conditioned reflex that you learned in early childhood. A calm mind helps us to broaden our perspective, to remain centred. That inner stillness promotes feelings of confidence and a sense of being more deeply in tune with ourselves. The most effective way to bring calm into our lives is to breathe more deeply and more powerfully, slowing each breath until we begin to release our physical and emotional tension and let the calmness bring a deeper sense of peace to our thoughts and feelings.

Let calmness become your normal state of being and tap into your deeper layers of creativity. Do it now. Do it every day. Let this sense of calm become a natural extension of everything you do.

3. Real energy. Feeling the Force of your natural energy source

Do you get an energy boost from caffeine? Do you ever feel the need to revive your spirits with coffee or caffeine-based drinks? Like many people, I enjoy the taste of good coffee but, if you need a better energy boost, try breathing more deeply and see what happens when you introduce more oxygen into your body. Deeper breathing calms you down, energises your body, improves your thinking and lifts your spirits. And it's totally free! I'm going to encourage you to breathe more deeply every day until it becomes a natural and life-enhancing habit that you perform without even thinking about it. It's so powerful, I'm amazed you don't need a prescription for it. When you take a deeper breath, remember to keep your throat relaxed. If your throat begins to tense, you've filled your lungs as much as you need and you can begin to exhale. If you breathe out powerfully and feel you are really emptying your lungs, you'll help your body to eliminate toxins and that will boost your energy and concentration levels. It's a totally free and naturally energising process and it feels wonderful.

Take a moment to try it right now and notice the difference you can make just by breathing a little more deeply. Try it every hour to awaken and refresh your mind and body. Feel the power flowing through your body. This is nothing more than your natural energy circulating through your system and your body will be smiling in appreciation.

4. Dreams. Accessing the profound insights and analysis of the subconscious super-computer

Hope I didn't wake you but it's time to welcome you to the importance of your dreams. Everything that happens in our lives is logged and recorded in our subconscious. Our conscious minds are occupied with the business of our daily existence but the vast resource of the subconscious is often neglected because it doesn't share a common language with our waking, conscious minds. Dreams provide a connection between the unconscious and conscious aspects of our minds. You can learn to recall your dreams as you wake up and even make notes about the symbolism that populates your dream world. Tell yourself before sleeping that you wish to remember your dreams at the moment of waking. The subconscious processes vast amounts of data and the conclusions are often revealed in dreams. This is a very powerful asset and extremely worthwhile in enhancing the quality of our lives, developing deeper understanding of ourselves and our circumstances, offering precise and timely insights into complex situations. Don't neglect your dreams. It's like having the latest Cray Supercomputer at your disposal and using an abacus. Dreams offer their highly personalised messages for your benefit and they are simply too important to neglect. Make a note to tell yourself to remember your dreams every night.

5. Fuel. Respecting your body's need for the most natural nutrition

A number of highly successful individuals that I've worked with held their bodies in very high esteem. They treated their bodies with obvious respect and consideration. That meant that they took good care of themselves and that included their diet. In fact most of them preferred to eat quite simply and modestly but always in accordance with their body's health requirements. It was one of the ways they stayed in shape and successfully dealt with the challenges that life would throw at them.

Food allergies create too many health problems today and that brings us to the important subject of food intolerance. The main culprits seem to be our old friends wheat and dairy products. The gluten in wheat and the casine in dairy products can produce a whole range of unpleasant reactions. We don't have to be allergic to these substances. We only need to be mildly intolerant. The effects can accumulate over the course of our lifetime until the body begins to display stronger reactions, eventually leading to a range of avoidable health problems.
The answer is to cut gluten out of your diet for a couple of weeks and see if your health improves. The same approach can be adopted for dairy products. This simple experiment can lead to an overall reduction in allergies, reduce skin problems and inflammatory diseases, improve breathing and, amongst many other benefits, boost your energy levels. If you suspect that you have any food intolerances, take steps today to reduce your intake of potentially allergic foods and increase your well-being. If it's true that we are what we eat, make today the day that you stop poisoning your body!

6. Positive Influences and the hidden power of our expectations.

Expectations shape the outcome of many events in our lives. Does that sound realistic to you? Do our expectations really influence the way that things happen in our lives? Well, we need to consider the fact that so much happens in our lives as a result of our interaction with other people. If we develop positive expectations in our relationships, this attitude shapes how people react to us. A positive expectation shapes our perception of the world around us. Our brains process data according to these patterns of expectation. When we adopt a positive frame of mind, people mostly react to us in a similarly positive way. This positive behaviour can influence the way people behave towards us and that in turn produces positive results. So our expectations can profoundly influence the outcomes in our lives. Your mission is to learn to expect positive results from friends, family, colleagues and situations. Learn to see positive potential in every condition and circumstance.

Programme your brain to expect really great, positive outcomes. The results can be both revealing and very pleasantly surprising. You might notice that your positive attitude becomes contagious, encouraging the people around you to share in the group spirit of achievement and success.

7. Rest 'n' Recovery. New habits to promote great sleep

Good sleep is a vital component of great health and a productive life but most of us haven't developed the right habits before switching off the lights at night. We need to create a space between the day's activities and our nightly rest period. This means no reading or television in the fifteen to twenty minutes before we go to sleep. Some experts recommend that we cut out all mental and visual stimulation for the three hours before we sleep but fifteen to twenty minutes should be enough time to switch off our mental activity and relax. That's the essence of the technique. We switch off and relax. We relax our bodies, let go of all the stress points, breathe deeply and let the mind settle into a natural and relaxed state. This calms everything down and prepares us for rest, recovery and recuperation. You'll notice the difference when you wake up feeling refreshed and ready to face anything the day might bring. That's a truly great way to improve the quality of your life and put you into a very positive frame of mind every single day.

8. Stretch It. A supple body support a flexible mind

Busy people, busy lives and not enough time to take care of everything. Does that sound like you? We are often asked if there is one thing that busy people can do to make the greatest contribution to health and well-being. Is there one simple answer to this complex question? From a physical perspective, the single most important contribution to your health, strength and well-being is flexibility. That's right. Flexibility.

People often give up exercise because it becomes painful. Lack of movement leads to a degeneration in joint mobility, a decline in strength and a marked reduction in overall physical and mental conditioning. This decline in exercise often leads to weight gain and movement becomes even more uncomfortable. The answer is in flexibility. Careful, gentle, daily stretching will enhance mobility even in the presence of injuries. Flexibility boosts mobility. If you can move, you can exercise. If you exercise, you get stronger, fitter, and healthier. Exercise boosts brain functioning.

The key to all these benefits is flexibility. A little stretching every day is one of the best long term investments in your health that you can make. You don't even have to stand up to stretch. You can make gentle, controlled moves while seated. Just make sure every move is pain free and let your natural potential to be a little more supple show up in your posture.

9. Creativity. Unleash the power of your Hidden Muse

Have you noticed how much healthier you look when you've been on holiday? Resting properly, relaxing, re-charging your batteries. If we consider the health benefits, we should be getting away for a break every month. Some productivity analysts would probably be horrified at the suggestion of more holidays but proper rest helps people to develop their creativity. Since holidays make such a welcome contribution to our well-being, we should find ways of bringing the holiday experience into our daily lives. This can be done by learning to release the stress that usually accompanies our daily working experience. Learning to relax more can help us to concentrate. Breathing more efficiently can stimulate our thought processes. Feeling well at work means fewer sick days. Unlocking our tension can boost productivity. So even if it isn't practical to take more holidays, learn to relax and bring that holiday feeling into work every day. The difference will surprise you. The health benefits alone more than justify the exercise. It's all in your mind, my friend. Use your mind to recreate that relaxed and energy-filled state of wellness that you bring back from holiday. And let every day rock!

10 Identity. Revealing the deeper sense of Self

Who are you? The fundamental problem we face as humans is that we really don't know who we are. This identity crisis creates inner tension and conflicting thoughts and feelings. We're conditioned from early childhood to play a series of roles that help us fit into family, society, culture and the work place. But do any of these roles really represent who we are? More importantly, if we really don't know who we are, how can we really expect to know who anyone else is? If there is one task in our lives that can resolve the really important questions about our existence, it is surely to understand at the deepest level who we are. This is a personal quest for which no adequate words exist. It is a process of realisation and understanding that shifts our awareness from the conditioned reflexes of early childhood into a richer and more meaningful expression of self. Ultimately, it is in answering this most demanding of questions that our purpose can be fully discerned and expressed. Meditation is the simplest way to explore the answer. Take a few minutes to slow down, breathe gently and relax. Let go of all the distractions around you. Let go of all the thoughts and feelings that float across the screen of your inner attention. Relax. Eventually your thoughts will become quieter and you'll notice a shift in your perception. This is the real beginning of meditation. And people who meditate live longer, healthier lives. Within the stillness you'll find all the answers you were looking for.

11. Nature. Re-connecting with the natural environment

Cities have transformed our experience of life and have come to represent our definition of advanced civilisation. Most of us live or work in cities so I recommend that you take time whenever possible to visit the countryside, to breathe the fresh air, listen to the birdsong and feel that healing connection to nature that helps to relieve stress and anxiety. There is such an extraordinary contrast between the grey concrete of city centres and the living array of colour that we find in the forest. People speak of the primordial energy of the trees, the healing energy of woodland, the calming effect of simply walking through the natural environment. Sometimes the contrast between the familiar surroundings of the home or the office and the natural beauty of a park or woodland can help you to see things from a different perspective. You discover other approaches to your immediate challenges. Make a date to spend a few hours in the countryside. Make it a regular trip. Give yourself a few hours to re-connect with nature. Enjoy the gifts of the natural world. It will equip you perfectly to survive the concrete jungle!

12. Parents.
Making peace with the first relationships and building a foundation for the future

You've got parents. That's how you got here. Our first relationships in life are with our parents. It is very important for our health and well-being to be at peace with this primary relationship. If we have problems or conflicts in this area, the problems will show up in every other relationship we try to build. Today is the day to fix this fundamental problem. We have a very strong motivator to find peace with our parents, to thank them for everything they did for us, to let go of any lingering conflicts and find true peace in this most basic dynamic that affects every aspect of our lives. It can be helpful to see our parents as people who did the best they could with what they knew. Let go of the need to judge them. Give thanks for their love and every other relationship in your life will benefit. Tell them you love them. Every day. Parents never get tired of hearing the words of love from their children.

13. Work. Finding the perfect way to express who you really are

Work is important. It dominates so much of our lives. It provides a way for us to earn a living and can offer a productive outlet for our energies. But do you define yourself mainly in terms of what you do every day? Is your job title the definition of who you are? I would hope that you can find a better and deeper expression of your identity that transcends the description of what you do at work.

Ultimately, our work should provide a natural extension of our deeper sense of who we are, a way to channel our abilities into a satisfying and productive way to lead our lives. It can be extremely worthwhile and revealing to ask ourselves if our work really provides the best outlet for our abilities. It's too easy to let the pressures and habits of our daily routine take over our lives but, if we really do not express ourselves satisfactorily, we build up tension and resentment that can erode our health and wellbeing.

So take a moment to ask yourself if you really are where you belong, doing what you should be doing, living the life that would allow you to express yourself completely. If you feel that you need to make a change, the only time to do it is now. If the change is too daunting, think about any skills that you might need to change your career and take classes. Make the change more comfortable. But make the change.

14. Chill. Unlocking the physical armour of your daily stress and learn to feel free

There's too much stress in our lives and part of transformation programme is to encourage you to release the daily accumulation of tension and learn to relax. Sometimes the day is just too busy, the pressure is constant and we become so completely engaged with our To Do list that we forget to take a moment to unlock our shoulders, breathe deeply and release the physical stress from our back and neck muscles.

So I want you to develop a fantastic habit for your well-being. At the top of every hour, remember to breathe deeply, relax your shoulders and give your body a moment or two to let go of the stress. It's so simple but so important for your health and well-being and you'll begin to notice the difference immediately. At the top of the hour - breathe and relax.

15. Awareness. Taking control of the inner realms of our thoughts and feelings

Physical exercise is a vital component in our health and wellness routines but we tend to neglect the importance of training the mind. Our thoughts and feelings seem to have a life of their own and refuse to follow our directions. But it is possible to exercise greater control over our thoughts and feelings by developing awareness, becoming conscious of how our thoughts arise and pausing to release them, learning to become more detached until we can begin to choose our thoughts more carefully.

This is the gateway to inner peace and a valuable tool for well-being. Begin gently by pausing for a moment and noticing what's going on around you. Notice the details. See everything that's happening and switch on your awareness. Breathe. Notice your thoughts and feelings and relax. This is the foundation of mindfulness and one of the gateways to liberation.

16. Getting down to the details. Building your personal priority List

What's missing from your life? Take a few minutes to relax and check your secret list of everything that you feel you'd like to have in your life. See if you can extend list to include fifty items. Begin with your material circumstances. When you've covered the obvious areas of physical comfort and security, list the things that you feel are missing in other areas of your daily experience. Remember, this list is not for sharing. It's for your eyes only. You're free to write down anything that occurs to you. You don't have to explain the list. It's a reference point for future developments. When you're finished, put the list somewhere safe. Take it out again in a week's time and read through it. See if anything needs to be changed. Now choose the items that you feel are essential but missing from your life and make a plan to bring them into your life. Then take action to make the plan a reality. Now.

17. Sleep. Maximising your daily down time to improve brain function

If you ever experience difficulty sleeping or feel that you could sleep better, there are many factors to consider that can influence your nightly rest. Diet plays its part. Poor circulation or lack of exercise can also interfere with your sleep. But most of us get into bed with all of the stresses and strains of the day on our minds and in our posture. So, when you go to bed tonight, try a different approach. We touched on sleep on Day Two but it's such an important subject that we'll remind you to follow these principles until they become a natural habit at bedtime.
First of all, don't read or watch television for the twenty minutes before you intend to sleep. If you over-stimulate your mind, it will be harder to fall asleep. Next, learn to relax your body, your entire body, from head to toe. Relax your face, neck, shoulders, limbs - everything. And breathe a little more deeply, gently inflating the chest, holding the breath for a second or two, then breathing out slowly and deeply. This simple process can help you to unwind, slow down, relax and prepare for sleep. Don't skip this essential ingredient in your Total Transformation Programme. Great sleep improves every aspect of our lives and the Programme won't deliver all of its amazing benefits unless you follow the powerful evening routine for great sleep.
You'll notice the difference when you wake up and feel more refreshed, more energetic, calmer and ready for whatever the day may bring you. A better night's sleep will help your mind and body recover from the pressures of the day and equip you to become more resistant to stress as each day unfolds. Learn to relax. And breathe.

18. Move. Appreciating the miracle of your body

Learning to relax is an essential component of our strategy for wellness but it's helpful to remember that our bodies also evolved to move. We spend so much of our time sitting down that it's easy to forget the importance of physical exercise. Our bodies really need to move. Movement is essential to our long term health. It's incredible to think that in the developed world most people rarely take any form of physical exercise. This contributes to health problems, including heart disease, obesity and a general deterioration in the quality of life. Most of the hyper-successful people I've worked with made sure they were in good shape and took regular exercise. The physical workouts helped them cope more effectively with stress, sleep better and get more done. Exercise enhances energy levels.

Our bodies need exercise to improve health, to reduce the effects of stress, to maximise our efficiency and improve our chances of having a long life. Our bodies are the only place we live in for the whole of our lives. Let's make a commitment to making our bodies as comfortable, healthy and happy as possible. We owe it to ourselves. Walking is a great way to kick start the body's potential for greater fitness. If you haven't exercised in a while, start gently and make sure you have no pain or discomfort. All you need is a pair of comfortable shoes and a place to walk. Not too difficult, eh? Begin today.

19. Flexibility.
Keep your joints in great working order and move more easily

I always encourage people to exercise, to move their bodies and develop better physical fitness. This is the only body we get to live in so we need to take great care of it. Being able to move without pain or discomfort is essential to long term health. Flexibility becomes even more important as we get older, so the sooner we start stretching, the sooner we enjoy the benefits. One of the best times to stretch is first thing in the morning as we get out of bed. Slow, gentle, relaxed movements, avoiding any painful positions, will set us up for the day and gradually build a strong base for long term suppleness. The secret is to take a few minutes to stretch carefully every day rather than over-stretching once a week. If you're patient and persistent, the results will surprise you and you'll develop a much healthier relationship with your body's strength, flexibility and well-being. You may find that persistent, nagging pains are eased as you begin to move your body and improve circulation. The body has remarkable powers to heal and repair itself. Switch on that potential with regular movement.

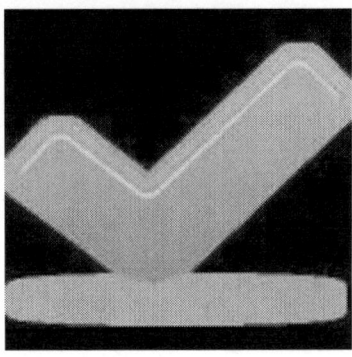

20. Your Word. Empowering the value of what you say

What is the value of your word? Do you give it without any sense of obligation or commitment? Do you say 'Yes' just to please people? When your word is strong, it acquires tremendous power. When you say 'Yes' with absolute conviction, you imbue your words with power. There is a real sense that having said 'Yes', whatever you've agreed to will come to pass. You convey certainty because your word has power. It's equally important to be able to say 'No' as well. Whichever words you choose, let them convey clarity and certainty. This simple act opens your life to deeper levels of expression and power. You will notice that you consider your words more carefully before using such a potent means of expression. When you feel the power in your word, you learn to exercise discretion and this change in your tone adds weight to your words. When you hear your word for the first time, imbued with power and clarity, you'll feel the change within you. It's beautiful.

21. Change. The irresistible power of choice

We often hear the expression 'Practise makes perfect' but this is not the case. Practise - makes permanent! If we always repeat the same actions, we can expect the same results. If we want things to be different, this implies that we must do things differently. If we always do things the same way, think the same thoughts, generate the same old familiar feelings, things will remain exactly as they are.

If we really want to create improvement and change in our lives, we have to change what we do, how we think and how we feel. Change the formula of your behaviour and you massively increase the probability of creating real change in your life.

Start by choosing how you want things to be. Choose how you want to feel. Then examine how your present actions are creating the outcomes in your life. This is the pathway to lasting improvement. Even small changes can produce extraordinary results.

22. Feelings. Taming our emotional habits

We are all deeply affected by our emotional energy. Our feelings influence how we relate and connect to other people and some would say that life is essentially an emotional experience. But our health and well-being are often at the mercy of our emotional responses. It's time to bring our feelings more closely under our control. It's time to learn to relax and give up the habit of responding instantly to every situation with a ready-made set of feelings. Pause for a moment. Ask yourself where all these feelings come from. Breathe deeply. Relax your shoulders. Find a calmer state of mind. Now you're learning to control your thoughts and your feelings. You are allowing yourself to feel stable, centred, calm and in control. This is the foundation of well-being. You no longer have to react the way you were taught as a small child. Now you have options. Your analytical, higher brain function can assess the situation objectively. Now you can choose better emotional responses and free yourself from your early conditioning. Forever.

23. Focus. Choosing to connect with positive outcomes

Our capacity to focus can produce an extraordinary intensity in our lives. What do you focus on? Do you find yourself thinking about the problems and difficulties in your life? Or do you deliberately look for the positive, affirming and fulfilling aspects of your daily experience? It's surprising how our consciousness filters out so much information and tends to notice the things we want to see. If we are intent on seeing difficulties, disappointment, problems and unhappiness, our awareness will narrow our field of vision to pick up these negative elements.

But if we look for positive data, things to celebrate, experiences that help the spirits soar and the heart to feel glad, it's amazing how our perception shifts to accommodate these positive and life-enhancing phenomena. We really are surrounded by good things. It's vital for our well-being that we learn to notice them. Winners always look for the signs of victory. Look out for them and you'll be surprised how often you find them.

24. Goals. Keeping your attention on your chosen destination

How do you react when problems show up in your life? Do the unexpected changes in your day push you off course? Do you feel angry or frustrated? Do you forget what you were aiming to achieve? It's during these moments of frustration that we must focus on our goals. Sometimes the problems are just part of the bigger picture and even though they may cause a change in direction, they must not deter you from your objectives.

So what is more important to you? The goal you've chosen for yourself? Or the pathway that takes you there? Don't mistake the pathway for the destination. Focus on your goal and though the pathway may twist and turn, you will most certainly reach your chosen destination. Learn to take problems in your stride, confident in your ability to reach your goals, and direct your energy towards the results that you intend to bring into our live.

25. Visualise. Use your imagination to lift your spirits

Are you affected by the weather? Most of us admit to mood changes according to the daily weather pattern and we all know how much easier it is to feel happy when the sky is blue and sun is shining brightly. But do you want to surrender your feelings to the lottery of the weather forecast?

The sun always shines, even when hidden by the clouds. Close your eyes. Imagine the sun shining brightly above you. Feel its warmth on your skin. Bask in its life-affirming radiance. Now you can feel the benefit of perfect weather all year round! Everything is a product of the way we filter the information around us. Even when you imagine the sunshine, you begin to feel better immediately. All it takes is a moment of visualisation and we can train the mind and body to respond instantly to our will. This is a powerful technique. Use it every single day until it feels completely natural.

26. Determination. Persistence paves the way to success and fulfilment

Success does not necessarily happen easily. It does not happen but accident. Super-successful individuals usually put this quality at the top of their hit list guaranteeing extraordinary results. Persistence is a critical factor in achieving our goals. If we could add one element to the daily equation of achieving our aims, it would be to keep on trying. Never give up. Keep your goal in front of you. All the time. Put pictures on your wall. Stick messages on your computer screen. Remind yourself at every level of what you want. Keep Post It notes in your purse. Broadcast the message to yourself all the time. Never get discouraged. Persist. Insist. Keep moving towards your goals every single day.

If one method or pathway doesn't take you where you want to go, don't change the destination. Hold fast to your heartfelt desires and be prepared to change the way you get there. Change the pathway, not the goal. It might take effort. It will certainly take commitment. But once you've visualised your destination, start living into it, imagining the great feelings you'll experience when you get what you've chosen. This engages the subconscious to work with you rather than against you. Take heart. Have courage. Keep going. Persist.

27. Appreciation and the Art of Being Grateful

We've all heard or read the expression 'The attitude of gratitude' and I'd like to remind you of the deeper value of this affirmation. When you cultivate a deep appreciation of all the wonderful things in your life, you focus less on what you think is missing and begin to value the gifts that life has brought you. You learn to appreciate the fruits of your efforts, your productivity and your success.

This feeling resonates in our subconscious and influences our thoughts, feelings and behaviour in a very positive manner. By turning our attention towards the positive elements in our lives, we begin to notice more reasons to celebrate our good fortune, we begin to feel more appreciative of the good things that make life such a rich experience. This leads to the discovery of more positive outcomes. Gratitude is one of the foundation stones of success. Find three reasons right now to be grateful. Write them down and feel the difference this makes to your day.

28. Generosity. Celebrate success wherever you find it

Success can be defined in many different ways. Your personal sense of success is very important but are you comfortable with other people's success? If you can celebrate and enjoy other people's success, you will become more open to success in your own life. A mean spirit impoverishes the soul. Give yourself the freedom to feel good about other people's success, celebrate their triumphs, promotions, victories and happiness. Then you will find it so much easier to recognise and celebrate these events in your own life. Be generous in all aspects of your life and life will be generous towards you. We grow in stature when we free ourselves from the pettiness of jealousy. Life looms larger when we free ourselves from the delusion that there isn't enough to go round. There's more than enough success for everyone. Confirm that fact by celebrating other people's achievements whenever you come across them.

FREE GIFT FOR YOU OUR READER

.....enjoy this free ebook and more!

http://www.onelifeblog.com/free-abundance-mini-ebook

29. Cash. Learning to be completely at ease with the power of money

Success in our culture is often measured in financial terms but how do you feel about money? What is your real relationship with cash? It might come as a surprise but many people feel very uncomfortable about money. It's a source of enormous stress. Most people feel they have too little and many don't even believe they deserve the money they get. So if you want to overcome your negative reactions about money - fear, doubt, anxiety, guilt - you have to start by feeling completely comfortable with money. This takes practice. A benevolent force with a smiling face that wants to help you in any way it can. It can be very helpful to think about money as if it were a living entity, something you can be friends with, something you can welcome happily into your wallet and into your life.

This change in attitude resonates in the subconscious and can produce remarkable results in your attitude and feelings towards cash. Make friends with money and take notice of the changes this makes in your life. You might be very pleasantly surprised.

30. Will and the extraordinary focus of a trained and flexible mind

Physical health can be dramatically improved by good diet and intelligent exercise, but do you take time to exercise your mind? Do you train your mind to think the thoughts that you want it to think? Does your mind obey you? Training the body is admirable. Training the mind leads to mastery of ourselves. We are very much the products of our early childhood conditioning. Learning to advance our mental and emotional potential means leaving these old habits behind so that we may develop more appropriate responses. Train the mind gently to follow your will and discover the power of focus, concentration and a broader, renewed perspective. Start gently with simple tasks. Learn to visualise a simple object with your eyes closed until you can see it with your mind's eye in every detail. Then learn to remove the image from your mind. Completely. Then bring it back. This unusual training develops extraordinary powers of mental focus and concentration. It's an ancient technique for developing the will and that is a gift of immeasurable importance in anyone's life today.

31. Freedom. The fuller expression of total success

Success comes in many forms and money is only one way of measuring it. Perhaps we should consider how much freedom we have rather than focusing exclusively on money. If you are free to enjoy your life, free to appreciate the great things that you already have, free to enjoy the love of friends and family, this is truly wealth beyond measure. Have you sacrificed your freedom and self-expression for an illusory notion of success? Take a moment to consider your freedom and how to create more space in your life to enjoy it. Greatness flows from this deep sense of appreciating the unmeasured treasures of your life. This creates a very stable platform for developing better ways of living and helps to incorporate change in a comfortable way that conforms to who we are and to what we truly desire.

32. Habits. Moving the framework of perception to change the universe

Are you tired of being angry? Well, anger certainly steals away vast amounts of our energy so it will most surely make you tired. But anger is nothing more than a habit, a way we learned to react when we were very young. A habit. Nothing more. A learned behaviour. So, if we want to, we can learn to behave differently. We can learn to catch ourselves getting angry and recognise the symptoms, the change in our posture, the shift in the rhythm of our breathing, the change in our thoughts and feelings. Then we can make small, subtle alterations and changes in our posture. Breathing more slowly, relaxing our shoulders, holding our breath for a second or two and suddenly - the conditioned reflex changes. Anger only exists because we fuel it with our emotional energy. Cut off the fuel and the anger ceases to exist. Instantly. Let's begin today by letting go of our anger and using our emotional energy to feel wonderful. Your body will thank you in so many ways. And the world around you will suddenly appear to be a very different place.

33. Hydrate. The magical power of H2O

Your body needs water. Lots of water. Not carbonated cans of poison. Water. You probably don't drink enough and your body may already be showing some of the signs of dehydration on a daily basis. You easily get used to the lack of water. You think it's normal. But it is not. You need water. So boost your health, detox your body, energise your mind and feel more alive by drinking water throughout the day. Starting now. A couple of liters a day should do the job. More if you work out regularly. There's a surprising amount of data on the subject that generally agrees on the virtues of adequate hydration. This might be more significant than you would suspect because the effects of environmental pollution add a considerable burden to our immune systems and drinking sufficient quantities of pure, fresh water is one of the simpler ways to rid your body of toxins.

34. Happiness as a way of experiencing the world

Amongst the world's sowers of wisdom the Buddha lent his understanding to every aspect of the human condition. One of his most popular quotes reminds us that happiness is not a goal, a product of doing or getting something. He suggested that it is a way of being. A powerful state of mind. This is a timeless reminder that enduring happiness cannot be found outside of ourselves. It is a state of being that flows from our hearts. It is not a temporary distraction from the cares of the world. It cannot be found in the fleeting experiences that occupy our senses. The inner sense of peace and calm that sets the world in a different framework is the foundation of health and well-being. It also lends itself to profound levels of creativity and this is one the great well springs of success. Become the happiness you seek and you will find it everywhere. This is another example of the timeless perception that the world reflects our inner state of being. As we experience the world through our emotional filters, the world becomes a mirror in which we see what is in our hearts. This is not some esoteric or mystical form of distraction from the world around us. It is an extremely powerful way to engage with life and successfully confront its constant array of challenges.

35. Awaken. Developing the power of perception

I was often surprised at the extraordinary level of perception that my mentors displayed. Sometimes it was like being with a gifted psychic. But they would always explain that they were simply looking, listening and perceiving what was in front of them. There was no secret. They simply noticed things that most of us ignore. They had learned to pick up the details. It gave them a huge advantage in any business environment.

The problem for most of us is that our senses our overloaded by constant distractions. Becoming more aware frees the mind from the habit of being overwhelmed. To practise the technique, find a quiet spot where you won't be disturbed for a few minutes. Sit comfortably, close your eyes and listen. Just listen. Become aware of all the sounds around you, some near, some further away. Breathe gently and notice the sounds. Most of the time we're so pre-occupied that we miss most of what's going on around us. Take a minute to slow down and begin to take notice of the sounds.

This is an ancient technique for helping us to feel centred and grounded, to feel a calming sense of detachment from the world around us. We begin this process by focusing our attention through the senses. This subtle shift in perception changes the way we perceive the world. This can produce some very pleasant surprises but its main function is to shift our habitual immersion in the distractions around us to a more focused yet detached overview of our environment. That's how we learn to become much more aware of what's really going on around us. That's when we begin to read the subtitles in people's conversations.

36. Negativity. Releasing yourself from the lifelong habit of negative feelings

Health check-ups are a great idea, a simple way to confirm that everything is fine or an early opportunity to address problems before they get out of hand. But do you ever give your thoughts and feelings a regular check-up? Are you aware of how toxic some of your thoughts and feelings can be? Feelings of anger, fear, stress, anxiety, irritability, jealousy, inadequacy can produce a range of unpleasant effects across the entire spectrum of your health and well-being. One of the fastest ways to deal with these feelings is to relax your shoulders and breathe more deeply, finding a calmer state of mind where the negative feelings don't have a chance to take root in your behaviour. Relax. Find the calm. Let go of the stress. Let the calm spread throughout your body. Unlock your jaw muscles. Ask yourself why you're feeling the way you do. Check your thoughts and feelings. Undo the habit of reacting immediately. Choose a better way to feel. Your health will benefit enormously from this simple process of learning to feel the way you want to feel.

Try it right now and feel the difference.

37. Action. Seize the moment. Seize the day

Don't delay. Procrastination eats up time and opportunity with equal indifference. One of the constant messages from my mentors was simply "So what are you going to DO about it?" It was always a call to action. The universe loves action. If you know what you really want in this precious life, take action right now to make your goal a reality. The first step is the most important. Take that step. Begin the journey. Take action. Do something to take you closer to your dream. Don't leave it until some perfect future moment. Start right now. There is only this moment in which you can do anything. So seize it. Use it. Start moving towards your goal. And remember to enjoy the journey. The act of taking that vital step can harness enormous potential to bring you closer to your goals and dreams. Do it now. Every single billionaire that I've met and worked with had to make that first move. Every success story begins with that first step. The missing ingredient is action. Action creates opportunities. One of my heroes was fond of saying "Action creates its own luck".

38. Influence. Touching the lives of everyone you meet

I've had some truly remarkable teachers. But, in reality, everyone is a teacher. We influence everyone around us with our thoughts, our words, our feelings and our behaviour. Whether we know it or not, we are always teaching.

We teach what we learn and we learn what we teach. When you recognise that your behaviour can influence those around you, you take on a deeper sense of responsibility for your actions. So choose your thoughts and feelings and behaviours carefully and be the teacher that makes a positive difference to the lives of those around you. And great teachers lead by example. Share your success. Acknowledge the help and support you receive. Pass it on to those you meet. Keep the wave of good experience rolling ever onwards and outwards, touching more and more lives with the power of the message. The message of real success.

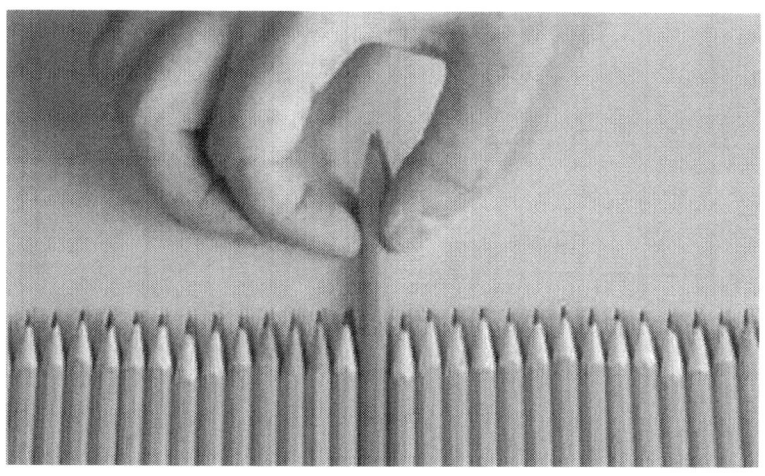

39. Choose. Becoming the origin of everything you feel

My teachers rarely wasted any energy on anger. There suggested that there was a sense of futility in losing one's temper. As if you lacked the belief in your power to take care of things.

The world is a mirror. Everything is really an extension of how you feel. Your perception is continually shaped by your emotional filters. No one has the power to make you feel anything without your permission. When someone 'makes you angry' the anger was already in your heart. Learn to choose your feelings, to focus on emotions that support your health, inner peace, creativity, success and wellbeing. The world is a mirror. Let it reflect the beauty within your own heart. Learn that when someone is angry, the anger is in their heart. How they feel is not about you. It's about their internal emotional landscape. When someone is angry, you know you don't have to share their anger. You are free to remain at peace. You are free to remain focused on your dreams, your goals, your personal fulfilment. Because that is what is in your heart. This awareness helps you to understand peoples' feelings in a different context. You no longer have to react according to other peoples' emotions.

40. Judgement. Banishing the veil of delusion that clouds our perception

Judgement clouds our values. It's a truly pernicious habit. We judge everything and everyone all the time, including ourselves. And the conclusions are rarely positive. Make a declaration today to give up judging, deciding who is good and who is bad. Begin this revolution in your perception by learning to accept yourself totally and unconditionally. You do not have to pretend to be perfect! There will always be areas that can be improved but we need first to know ourselves. Not with judgement but with compassion. As we learn to accept ourselves, to let go of the guilt and disappointment, we may learn to accept others more easily and this brings greater harmony into our lives, eliminating stress from our relationships, warming our hearts, freeing up essential energy to focus on our success. It becomes so much easier to be with others and to feel completely comfortable in most circumstances. Because you're learning to be comfortable with yourself.

41. Tuning in and tuning out

Relaxation is an art and a science. A method of slowing down the stress response and regaining the natural composure that enhances your creativity. A way to breathe more deeply and change your perspective, see the world and your surroundings in a different light. This is how you maintain natural control when the going gets tough. This how you access your creativity instead of your fear.

So relax your shoulders and turn down the stress. Breathe slowly, gently, deeply and the world changes around you. Switch off your fear. Regain your composure. Notice now what's going on around you. Feel the inner stability. One of our greatest challenges as individuals is to learn how to let go, to release our fear, our anger, our habits. Letting go of the past so that we may create a future that fulfils our deeper requirements and illuminates our goals with the beacon of assured success.

Take a moment right now to breathe, to relax and let go of absolutely everything you don't need.

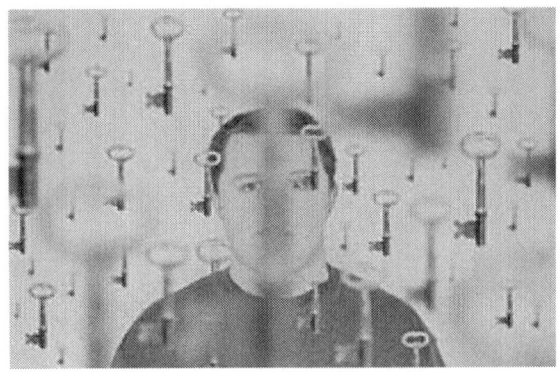

42. Identity. The power of being who you really are

Sometimes we forget who we really are. So much of our lives get caught up in playing roles. We have to conform to the demands of our work, our families, society and eventually we begin to lose our deeper sense of identity. You know when this is happening because you become more stressed. You forget how capable you are. You close your eyes to your abilities. You abandon your potential. That's why so many people take the inevitable setbacks so seriously and abandon their dreams and goals. They deny their true potential. They slip into an old, redundant role of pretending to be incapable.

But today is the perfect day for remembering who you really are. A perfect day to feel the power within you, to let go of your fear, release the past, let your deeper sense of self bubble up to the surface. And feel the power, the creativity and your natural ability to make a positive difference to the world around you. Feel the determination and the inner strength that tell you that you will make it. Know it in your heart and it shall be so.

43. Control flows so easily from your posture

Whatever is happening in your life, however you might be feeling, you can influence your thoughts and emotional state by relaxing your shoulders. We always respond to the position of our shoulders. Relax the neck, trapezius and shoulder muscles and the stress slips away from your posture. You can breathe more easily, more deeply. Your fear evaporates. Your perspective shifts. All from a simple change in your shoulder position. Try it right now. Going to a meeting? Having an interview? Making a presentation? It doesn't matter what you're doing. Relax your shoulders and you'll feel so much more confident and at ease. This is one of the simplest and yet most effective ways to take control of how you feel. Relax your shoulders and let go of the tension. Feels good, doesn't it? Practise this technique every hour during the day until feeling relaxed and powerfully centred becomes your natural condition.

44. Obstructions. Obstacles or excuses?

Have you noticed that your pathway always seems to be strewn with obstacles? Obstacles are a natural part of daily life but how we perceive them is a clear reflection of how we see the world. The more emotional energy we invest in the obstacles, the stronger they appear. Rather than focusing so much of your energy on why you are not making progress, focus instead on what you want. Concentrate your emotional energy on the outcomes that you most deeply desire. Learn to feel how good it will be to find yourself in exactly the situation and circumstances that you've chosen for yourself. Successful people focus on their goals.

Obstacles are not the goal. There may be many ways around any obstacle that blocks your way but it's helpful to remember that you really only need one way to get round it, go over it or move through it. Don't let the obstacles define your life, your dreams, your goals, your possibilities. Move your heart towards the results you want and your life will move in this direction. Start now. It's the only moment where you can truly begin to initiate the changes you seek.

45. Problems. The ability to place difficulties into their wider perspective

Life will always present us with problems, trials and challenges but it's vital for our wellbeing to maintain a positive and highly directed perspective. This means learning to focus on the more positive aspects of life, including the rewards we can expect when we deal with our problems successfully. In other words, if we only focus on our difficulties, that's all we will see. But if we focus on the areas outside of our problems, we can create a more balanced, less stressful view of our circumstances and this enhances our creativity and our potential to solve problems. Our focus influences our perspective; focusing on negative issues reinforces our perception of the world as a hostile and difficult environment. Focusing on the positive aspects of our life encourages a healthier, positive and empowered approach to our daily challenges and helps to reduce stress whilst boosting our well-being. So if you really want to engage more powerfully with the events that surround you, learn to recognise the brighter, more positive aspects of your situation rather than simply seeing the difficulties. You may find the problems are still out there, but your power to deal with them will be deeply enhanced.

46. Letting go of the past and discovering a brilliantly illuminated future

The past can cast a long and painful shadow on our lives, especially when we consider how often our feelings and sensitivities have been hurt. But the past is only really perceived by the shifting lens of our emotions and it is not a reliable way to deal with past events. Our emotions colour our experience of the past until the original events become distorted and blurred, unrecognisable and easily pressed into service to justify our egocentric view of the world. Our challenge is to learn to let go of the past. Completely. To free ourselves from these stories of what did or did not happen so that we can be free to choose a future that fulfils our dreams and potential. Successful people do not let the shadows of the past influence the future. Letting go of the past is a truly liberating experience and an essential step on the pathway to complete well-being and the expression of a harmonious and integrated personality. It also creates the space for a totally new and ferociously successful life, for the fulfilment of your wildest dreams.

47. The Core. Making the most of your inner strength

You're human and you have a body. It's a truly remarkable product of the evolutionary process and your body has incredible potential. Nature was generous enough to endow us with very strong core muscles. But due to the way we sit and stand, we rarely use them. So strengthen your core muscles. If you suffer from lower back pain, this is one of the best things you can do to relieve the discomfort and live a life free of back pain. Our core abdominal muscles are incredibly tough, strong and capable of extraordinary endurance. When they're engaged, they help to release stress and tension from our vulnerable lower backs and support the body in the most natural way possible. Our first objective is to banish pain from our bodies so that we can move, stretch and exercise with maximum comfort. Once we can move easily, exercise becomes easier and we can work on our fitness whilst reducing the chance of injury. This begins with our deep abdominal muscles. Nature gave them to us for a purpose. Let's put them to work right now. The Pilates revolution is today's wake up call to learn to use our core strength.

48. Stripping away the illusion of protective armour

Here's some eminently practical advice to help you get in touch with your stronger, more powerful self: relax! As we've recognised on several occasions, we learn to be defensive at a very early age and this habit influences our behaviour for the rest of our lives. The physical effects of this defensive attitude can be seen in our tense shoulder, neck and back muscles, the tension in our chests and the difficulty in breathing deeply. This defensive stress has been called 'body armouring' and this description sums up the problem perfectly; we go through life wearing layers of protective armour - physical, mental and emotional defences that create the illusion of being protected.

The challenge for us is to stop, breathe and begin to remove the armour, to peel away the false layers of security that shape our behaviour so that we may discover the power that lies beneath the delusion. It isn't a comfortable experience to relax our guard. We naturally feel vulnerable but this is how our fears trap us. Learn to let go. Release the fear and tension. Breathe more deeply and experience the revolution of living beyond the shadow of your fear. It's the first step towards freedom and a return to a more natural, beautiful and healthy way of living.

49. Isolation. Being totally present with other people

Many people in our society suffer from a sense of separation and isolation from everyone else. This might explain some of our stranger behaviours and apparent indifference to the people around us. But this sense of disconnection is based on an overly defensive attitude, something most of us learn in our early childhood. We learn to be fearful and protective, to look for problems where they don't exist, to mistrust everyone, including ourselves. This isn't a healthy way to experience life. This overly defensive behaviour denies us so many opportunities to experience happiness and share in the wonder of other people. We don't have to abandon our common sense and adopt a careless and naive approach to our fellow human beings but a more positive set of expectations can produce a much more positive level of interaction with others and this makes life so much more pleasant and comfortable for everyone.

50. Acceptance. The power of being you

Feeling good about yourself is not a luxury. It's an essential part of well-being and learning to accept yourself is an important part of discovering your deeper potential for happiness and fulfilment. This doesn't mean that we simply surrender to our faults and imbalances and unhealthy behaviours. But if we feel inspired to improve our lives, it's very helpful to begin by accepting ourselves as we are and using that sense of calm and positive self-awareness as the foundation for any changes we wish to make. We create far too much pressure in our lives by measuring ourselves against some artificial standard of perfection. We don't have to be perfect. Making mistakes and getting things wrong are normal aspects of our human condition. Perfection is an abstraction. Well-being is something that we can feel and experience as a healthy and uplifting aspect of every moment of our lives. So look in the mirror and smile and enjoy the feeling of well-being that follows. Pretending to be someone else simply takes up far too much of your time and energy. And these resources are better deployed on behalf of your evolving plans for success and complete self-expression.

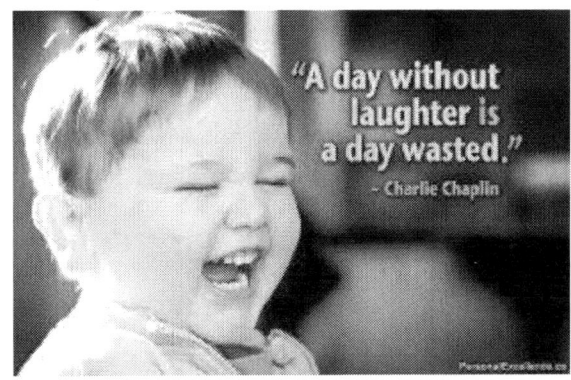

51. Laughter. The ultimate weapon to wield against the illusion of fear

There is a wonderful story that the Angel who stands at the right hand of God is responsible for laughter. This is a powerful reminder that humour is the great antidote to so many potentially stressful situations. We seem conditioned to take everything far too seriously and this over-emphasis on the importance of every event overwhelms us with stress, tension and a constant state of defensiveness. Laughter dispels fear. Laughter breaks the chains of stress. Laughter helps us to put things into perspective. Humour is one of the greatest gifts that humans can share and we would be much happier in our lives if we remembered to smile more, relax and laugh out loud at the absurdity of our fears. Less fear allows for bolder steps and, as I'm sure you know, Fortune most definitely favours the bold.

52. Perspective.

We are social creatures, connected to everyone around us and influenced by the behaviour of the people we encounter. But we sometimes become too focused on our own problems and difficulties and this is where our connection to other people can provide a timely antidote. If we move our attention from our obsession with our own problems to the problems of others, and try to help others in their difficulties, this change of focus often helps us to resolve our own challenges. At the very least, this change in perspective helps to put our problems into a broader context, moving us beyond the limitations of our circumstances whilst developing a sense of empowerment. If we can help others, we can help ourselves, and this positive reinforcement gives us the confidence to overcome our difficulties and move on to fresh opportunities. It's a frequent refrain in this guide to successful living but - the universe loves it when we take action.

53. Power and the absolute intensity of the trained Will

I've known some highly focused and intense individuals, super successful people with incredible will power. Training the will is one of the most neglected disciplines in our culture. We've inherited an archaic view of the will as some domineering force that overcomes all opposition by strength and raw aggression. But, if you learn to engage its incredible power, the will is an instrument of great subtlety. Learning to engage it with gentleness and restraint reveals the playful nature of this often forgotten faculty. It can become so powerfully focused that it will produce extraordinary results in your life. When you direct your will, it is almost effortless. Yet it is as natural and unobtrusive as your breathing. We train it by using it initially for small things, simple acts where we declare what we will do - and it happens. This leads to more powerful statements of intent where your will automatically creates the focus to achieve whatever goal you've chosen. Your will. A powerful and positive force for direction and change in your life. Switch it on right now. Feel the first hints of its intensity. Now turn it towards something worthwhile.

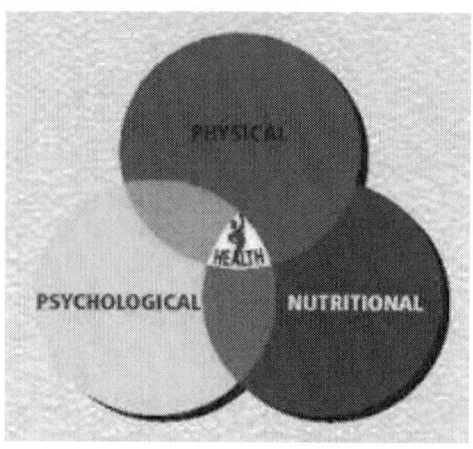

54. Habits and the Way of Total Health

Your body is a truly remarkable place to live. It's the only place you live in throughout your entire life. So let's make your body as comfortable, healthy and efficient as possible. We need to be mindful of what we eat, respecting our individual body types and choosing foods that support our health and well-being. We need to respect our bodies and give them every opportunity to function at peak efficiency. We need to keep our bodies hydrated and ensure we get plenty of rest. All these things may seem obvious but when we're busy, stressed and under pressure, we forget these essential ingredients to health and the quality of our lives is impaired. Most of our behaviour is based on well established habits. So choose habits that promote your well-being and feel free to question any habits that have a negative impact on your health and happiness. It's your responsibility. It's your body. Make a decision right now to take really good care of it.

55. Get creative.

Variety is the spice of life and creating contrasts in our routines supports overall creativity. It's too easy to spend too much time focused on work or slumped passively in front of a TV or computer screen. Think about something you'd like to make. Find the skill that's necessary to make something. Buy a book or take classes to acquire the skills but learn to do something creative. This is a very positive way to enhance your latent creativity and teaches the brain to function more productively. It's incredibly satisfying to see the finished results of your efforts, to hold something you've created, to refresh or learn new skills. It doesn't have to be a masterpiece. It's the process of creating something yourself that produces the most satisfaction. Choose something today and get started.

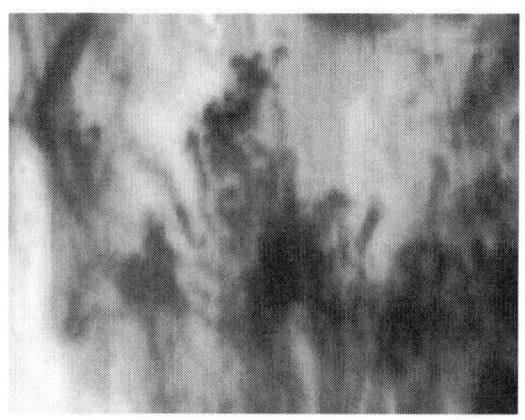

56. Sleep and the art of passive refreshment

Sleep is such an important part of our lives that I return to the subject on a regular basis. If you've been exercising your will, this is a great area to experiment. Let's remind ourselves that it's essential to relax before you go to sleep. Tell yourself firmly and gently that you are going to sleep deeply and peacefully. Use your will as an instrument of intent and you'll wake up feeling wonderful and full of energy. Tell yourself that you love the comfort and security of your bed. Calmly suggest a time to yourself for waking up.

These techniques harness the power of the mind and the will and provide clear instructions and expectations for the body. This simple exercise reinforces the connection between your will and your body. The result is a much better night's sleep and that gives us more energy, focus and concentration during the day. Try it tonight. Make it a regular part of your night time routine and feel the difference of a great night's sleep every night.

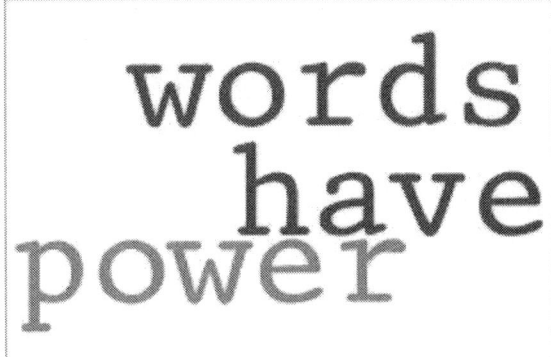

57. Words and the language of powerful intent

Language forms a vital link between the world of our thoughts and imagination and the way we connect to the outside world. But have you noticed how easy it is to use negative language rather than positive expressions? We say 'should', 'might' and 'maybe' rather than 'will', 'shall' and 'definitely'. Shifting our language into a more positive framework helps to focus our energy on precise outcomes and encourages our minds to overcome obstacles and concentrate on achieving our goals. Conditional expressions reveal an expectation of failure. Clear statements of intent reinforce our will to achieve whatever we set out to do. Become more aware of the words you use. Watch out for negative, weakening words that dilute your power to fulfil your goals. Choose positive, powerful expressions and feel the difference in your outlook. Let your daily use of language become a key to success, fulfilment and well-being. When you find a clear expression of intent, reinforce the power of your words by writing them down. Add the date and time to the note and sign it to authenticate your intent.

58. Greatness is the natural human condition

Greatness is a perfect expression of human potential. It's a beautiful extension of our capacity for growth and self-realisation, a metaphor for complete success. If you aspire to express the greatness within you, you have to recognise the greatness within everyone else too. Greatness does not exist as an isolated quantity that can only be found in the hearts of the few. Greatness is a constant facet of the human condition and when we begin to glimpse this greatness in the people around us, we begin to recognise the greatness that is in our hearts too. Pause for a moment in your busy life and look for the greatness that dwells in the hearts of everyone. See it and give thanks for this pure expression of human potential. It's all around us. It's an essential component on the great equation for total success and contentment.

59. Acceptance and gratitude for the miracle of your body

You need to develop a much healthier relationship with your body. This is a subject we touch on regularly because it's so important to our programme for total well-being. We're surrounded by images of 'perfect' bodies that only exist within the realm of a computer program. This constant exposure to artificial standards of health and beauty creates very negative reactions when we take time to consider the state of our own bodies. We can never measure up to these artificially enhanced images and this is potentially harmful to our health, happiness and well-being. So start the day by remembering to smile at yourself in the mirror. It might feel uncomfortable at first but it helps to establish a more co-operative relationship between your body and your subconscious. Learning to appreciate the miracle of your body, despite what you might feel it looks like, is a fundamental step towards healing, restoring, rejuvenating and strengthening your body. So let's show some positive appreciation for the home we live in for the entire duration of our lives: our bodies.

60. Liberation and the magnificence of letting go

One of the underlying causes of depression and anxiety in our society is the conviction that we really are not in control of our lives. Many people suffer from a feeling of being powerless, that they can't make a difference to their lives or circumstances. This feeling of helplessness leads to a form of mental and emotional slavery, a sense of being trapped and imprisoned in our lives. The moment you realise that you and only you are in control of your circumstances is a moment of true revelation. The energy we use to bind ourselves to the delusion of helplessness is the same energy we can use to set ourselves free. This is beyond some theoretical notion of freedom. This is a direct and powerful realisation that you really can experience extraordinary levels of liberation right now at this very moment. Relax your shoulders. Change your posture. Breathe. Your body responds immediately to these positive inputs. Your thoughts and feelings respond to your new posture and deeper breathing and you've suddenly created an extraordinary change in your emotional and mental well-being. The power is within in you. It always was. Use it for the most positive outcomes. Know that you are in charge of your destiny and start to make choices that improve your life and circumstances. If you want things to change, it's up to you.

61. Get in shape and invest in your fitness and longevity

People expect me to encourage them to exercise and make time for physical fitness but it's often a surprise when I advise runners to give up their sports for a while and learn to improve their posture. I've known many Marathon enthusiasts and long-distance runners over the years and most of them have created long term damage and injuries to their joints because of bad posture. That's a regrettable and unnecessary side effect of the way most people run today. It's important to remember that humans evolved to run. It's an essential product of our ancient evolutionary past to be able to jog long distances to find food. But the key to injury-free running is to use the body the way that Nature intended. That means minimal pressure in the lower back. Flexibility. Relaxed shoulders. Natural tension in the deep abdominal muscles and a smooth, easy running style. I'll continue to advise people to move their bodies but only when we're confident that they can run without pain, injury or unnecessary strain.

Let's respect Nature's wisdom and celebrate the miracle of our bodies by exercising with care and complete awareness of whatever we're doing.

62. Blame and the failure to take full responsibility

Winners take responsibility for their lives. This is a very useful distinction because it's so tempting to blame someone else for our problems. We blame our parents, our teachers, our friends, our enemies, society at large or anyone we can think of - anyone except ourselves. We've talked before about the importance of taking responsibility for our lives. Giving up the habit of blame is another important step in the process. We can't change the past. It's happened. It's over. Now move on.

Our focus must move towards the future, towards the future that we absolutely want for ourselves. When we let go of the habit of blaming others for who we are and what we do, we instantly feel the freedom of taking complete responsibility for our lives. This new sense of personal freedom creates the space for us make positive and lasting changes in our lives. We choose. No one else gets to make those choices for us. Certainly not anyone from the past! Let's celebrate our new freedom and unchain ourselves from the past. Forever.

63. Harness the Force of the Focused Mind

The mind is an extraordinary gift. Its powers can be harnessed for our well-being or for our detriment. The way we use our minds impacts directly on everything we experience in life. Our health, our happiness, our prosperity, our relationships - everything revolves around the emotional patterns in our thoughts and feelings. This power is a fact. We don't have to decide if it's real. We use it all the time. The real choice is to decide how to use this incredible force for our benefit. If there is any aspect of your life that you're not happy with, look at the thoughts and feelings that spring up when you focus on this issue. The answer to your problems is usually to be found in your own mind. That's why we need to let go of the disabling expressions 'I can't', 'I mustn't', 'I won't', 'it's not possible' and learn to express ourselves only with positive, enabling language. Your mind will understand. Your mind will respond to this change in how you want to think. The vast resource of your mind will start to work for you. And your life will start to get better.

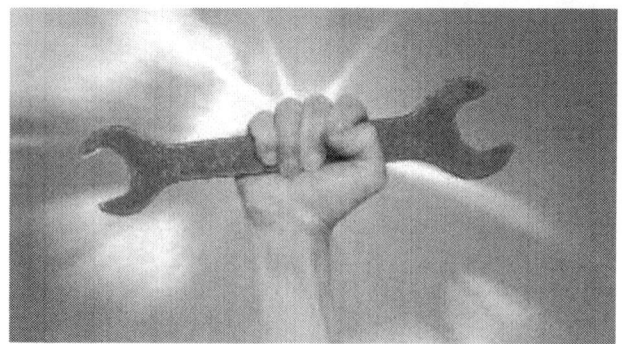

64. Fixing yourself by giving permission to get better

Anyone who's ever been involved in healing will know that the power to aid recovery comes from the person who needs the healing. It's easy to talk of healers as if they have some divine gift but all natural healing is a result of the sick person tapping into their own power. Sometimes the healer acts as a catalyst. But the miracles that sometimes attend recovery from very serious illnesses flow from the person who is being healed. This is helpful to understand because it ensures we never ignore the power that resides in everyone.

Power is not an elitist badge of honour. It is a universal characteristic. Recognising it in everyone we meet is essential for our balanced growth. We are more accustomed perhaps to the nuisance of colds and 'flu and these conditions are simple mechanisms for forcing individuals to slow down and rest! Not much comfort when you have a cold but a useful way to consider these minor complaints and a sign from your body for you to get more rest. The body has wisdom far beyond words.

65. Cosmos and the appreciation of the Infinite

Starlight is magical. One of the joys of visiting locations which are free from pollution is the wonder of a star-filled sky. The sense of receiving light that has travelled unimaginable distances across the vastness of space helps to put our worries into perspective. The scale of the universe simply exceeds the limits of our imagination by an incalculable degree and moves our perspective from the obsessively warped focus of the ego to the transcendence of self. An evening in the company of the stars is a delightfully relaxing yet exhilarating experience, a way to step beyond the limits of our daily concerns and breathe in the majesty of the universe. Science may explain much of what we perceive as we probe deeper into the mysteries of astronomy but it can never dilute the simple joy of feeling that essential connection to the wonder of the night sky. Take a moment to appreciate the stars. They're priceless. They're free. They're always there.

66. Take another shot at your personal Hit List.

It's time to review your list of things that you felt were missing from your life. Take a moment to relax in a quiet, private place and read through your list. If anything strikes you as irrelevant, cross it out. If you've produced something that was formerly missing in your life, cross it out. Add anything that now seems important to you. Any changes are evidence that your list is evolving. Choose one or more items that you feel you can work on right now and highlight them for action. What do you need to do to have the things that are missing? Write down your intentions and put the list away for a another week or so. And take action. This private power list is one of the tools that very successful people use to keep track of their goals and intentions. It soon becomes a tacit witness to your achievements as you complete or achieve each task and move purposefully on to the next one. Go on. Take action.

67. You and the need for private space

Our lives are often dominated by the needs of work, family, children and a host of competing responsibilities. You to find some time just for you. It isn't selfish and it doesn't detract from your other duties but it will help to restore some much-needed balance to your life. Set aside some time for yourself every single day. Use it for whatever you want. Meditate. Dream. Think about your goals. Think about your own needs and welfare. Make this an important part of your daily routine. Set aside time to make plans for yourself. Focus on you and use your special time to consider how to improve your well-being. Let the seeds of creativity germinate in your imagination and help you fulfil your individual needs, opening up greater possibilities for self-expression and personal fulfilment. As you take care of others and your daily responsibilities, take time to care of you as well. And whatever plans emerge in your mind, be sure to write them down. Make a simple declaration that you are going to do whatever is necessary to fulfil your plan. And take action.

68. Belief and the irresistible drive of your vision

Do you believe in yourself? If you want to make progress, build a better life, develop greater well-being and move yourself to a happier state of existence, you really have to believe in yourself. It's clearly very helpful to have people in your life who also believe in you and support your goals but the strongest source of support has to begin with your own beliefs. It begins with your belief that you can do whatever you want to do. Believing in yourself is a state of mind. It's something we need to practise every day until it becomes a natural reflex. It doesn't matter whether you had supportive parents or not as a child. The time for self-belief is right now. This very moment. We had to learn our doubts and limitations as small children and those habits have been with us for long enough. Today we need to learn the power of self-belief and feel the difference this change in attitude produces. When you believe in yourself, you'll smile with the knowledge that you can truly accomplish your dreams.

Self-belief is the beginning of so many wonderful things. Make it one of your best habits.

69. Balance and the art of making time for the important things in your life

Our mission is to create success across every area of your life. One of the principles that should guide all of us is to seek balance in each aspect of our daily lives. That means avoiding extremes. People are often drawn to extreme diets or extreme regimes to correct their perceived problems but our bodies naturally seek a state of balance. Life is a precious gift that deserves to be cherished and enjoyed. Giving yourself permission to enjoy things is extremely healthy and promotes a very positive feeling of self-worth. When you value your body, you naturally treat it with the care it deserves and avoid things that cause harm. But enjoyment is a powerful aspect of the human condition and when you opt for extreme regimes, you might be hurting yourself as a subtle form of self-punishment. Celebrate the gift of life and enjoy your body he way that nature intended. Make time for your friends and for your family. I've worked with incredibly successful people who scheduled time in their diaries for these vitally important parts of their lives, setting aside precious time to be with their partners and children. They insisted that it was a sign of a truly successful human being and I could see the wisdom in their choices.

> Laughter is the fireworks of the soul.
>
> ~ Josh Billings ~

70. Laughter is just so wonderfully good for you.

It's a fact. Laughter has great health benefits. How do you feel when you laugh? Exactly. It's a simple way to feel better and put many of life's challenges into perspective. And life is surely a most serious business for most people. Every day brings its share of new problems, obstacles and difficulties. We might not be able to make our problems disappear with laughter but seeing the funny side to a problem changes our perspective and takes the fear out of our responses. Laughter can enhance our creativity and help us to see problems in a wider, less threatening context, enabling us to find the best way to deal with the issues without becoming enmeshed in fear and anxiety.

Laughter is your best friend. Laughter can oxygenate the brain, release endorphins and boost your creativity and well-being. Let's treasure laughter and welcome it into our lives as the gift that helps us to deal more lightly with life's daily challenges.

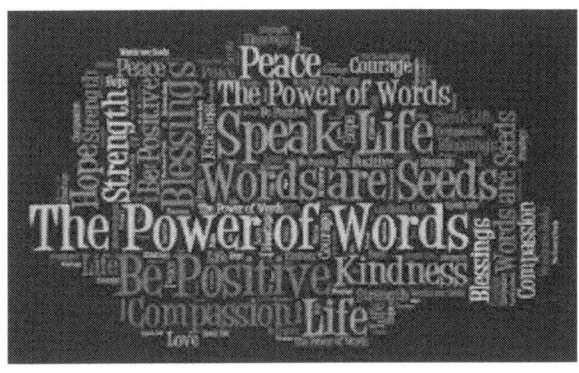

71. Vocabulary and the power of our words

The language we use is very important in framing our expectations of life. It might be a surprise to learn that when you use expressions such as 'I can't', your body becomes physically weaker, even when you're speaking about non-physical activities. This phenomenon even applies when you make simple, truthful statements. If you were to say 'I can't walk on water', there is obvious truth in the statement but the phrasing still affects us physically. It's a fascinating curiosity but an important element in our quest for healthier, fitter and happier lives. Negative expressions affect us at all levels. Declarations such as 'I can't' seem to rob us of our initiative and limit our creativity.

How much better could our lives become if we learned to become more aware of these seemingly harmless but negative expressions? How much more capable would we feel if we looked in the mirror every day and stated 'I can'? I'm inviting you to try the exercise, even though you might feel a little self-conscious at first. Look yourself in the eye and tell yourself ten times that you can do something and really mean it. Notice the changes in your posture. Notice the change in your confidence. Feel the energy. Feel the excitement.

Do it every day until it's part of your everyday behaviour. Make it a part of yourself.

72. Inspiration.

How often do we feel truly inspired by the attitudes and examples of very positive people? I've felt the force of this kind of intense positivity almost like a physical pressure in the room. Positive attitudes are like a breath of fresh air. How often do we feel the opposite? That the world is conspiring against us? How often do we react to our daily problems as if the universe was somehow trying to make life more difficult? It is certainly possible and very helpful to learn to see every situation as a welcome opportunity to learn. Every problem we encounter provides an opportunity to learn, to overcome shortcomings and develop a healthier, stronger and more positive attitude. Choose to believe that the universe is working to make everything better. That's a rare and astonishing approach to life's challenges but it helps us to see advantages where most of us would see only problems. Theuniverse is conspiring to make my life better'. What a wonderfully positive attitude to apply to every situation we meet. Print out the phrase and put it somewhere where you can see it every day. This is a singularly powerful tool for improving your life at every level.

73. Compromise and the obvious evidence of a truly successful life

One of the most revealing questions we can ask about any aspect of our lives is to look at ourselves in the mirror and demand to know whether we are happy. It's a very simple question. We can only answer yes or no. Are you happy? Be honest with yourself. Is your life matching your expectations? Does your life make you smile? It's a highly relevant question to help you understand where you're making compromises in your life. If you're not happy with a situation, that can only mean that your circumstances don't meet your expectations. Where can you make changes that will improve the situation? What's getting in the way?

The moment you begin to believe that you can really have profound happiness in your life, you initiate changes in your perception and subtle changes in your behaviour. You start to do things a little differently and change naturally follows, opening up the possibility of greater and sustained happiness in your life.

74. Enough effort can move a mountain

If you want anything worthwhile to happen in your life, you have to be prepared to make the effort. You have to be prepared to work for what you want, whatever your goal or intention may be. You cannot pay someone else to do your push ups for you. We all need help, of course. We need encouragement and support but the main effort must come from ourselves. Sometimes it must be tempting to wait for others to make things happen for us but that can only lead to disappointment. Take the initiative. Make the effort. It's another of those messages that the super successful would repeat like a sacred mantra. When you don't have effort, there's nothing to channel or direct. Effort is the fuel that powers the project to success. Be prepared to fail along the way too but be prepared to renew your efforts to make your goal a reality. It can be powerfully reassuring to know that ultimately, the main catalyst for change and improvement in your life is you. Take action. Make the effort and don't give up. Your future and your goals are in your hands. They always were.

75. The world you create is largely in your head.

Our minds are wonderfully complex areas for exploration but are too often conditioned to behave in set patterns that reflect our earliest experiences. We know that our perception can be deceived by optical illusions but we don't always recognise that our emotions can also be deceived by false impressions. We usually see life in the terms that we expect. Our perception delivers a view that conforms to our beliefs. Change your belief and you change your perception. I hope you'll be motivated to explore this idea to the full and create a revolution in the way you perceive the world and everyone around you. Engage your thoughts and feelings fully in the campaign to have a wonderful life and make the appropriate effort to turn your dreams into reality. And dream big!

76. Victory and the reassuring log of your achievements and successes

Life can provide more than its share of disappointments but one of the ways to counter the emotional side effects of defeat and setbacks is to keep your very own victory log. This is a record of everything you've ever achieved. But be warned! Once you start taking note of all your achievements, the list will seem endless. The surprise is that we are conditioned from childhood to respond to setbacks with very strong feelings that reinforce our fears and doubts but very few people feel comfortable celebrating their achievements and enjoying their successes. We need to correct this imbalance in our lives and a victory log will serve the purpose perfectly. List everything that you've achieved. That means everything. Enjoy the confidence that flows from a simple admission that you really are a capable and creative individual. It will work wonders for your self-esteem and put a well-deserved smile on your face! Some of the world's most successful CEOs keep this kind of log on hand to reinforce their confidence when they go into meetings. Feeling successful is a potent resource to deploy in any situation.

77. Inner joy and the pathway to internal calm, serenity and abiding peace

Happiness is an elusive state that we all seek in our daily lives and it's often related to specific circumstances, places, events or people. We seek pleasure and we avoid pain. That's how we mostly operate. Our normal state of happiness is therefore extremely limited and largely tied to external, temporary phenomena. But there is a deeper state of happiness that arises from consciously deciding to look for this powerful, amplified feeling within our hearts. Learning to feel happiness at this deeper level means learning to undo our old feelings, training our emotions to follow our will and understanding the enormous freedom that follows from choosing how we feel rather than allowing circumstances to dictate our mood. If this deeper state of happiness becomes our normal, daily state of being, the body responds with greater levels of well-being and we learn to feel precisely the way that we wish to feel. Does this eliminate spontaneity in our emotional responses? No. It opens our experience to richer levels of powerful and beneficial feelings. We become entirely available for happiness that endures and sustains us.

78. Challenging the familiar mental landscape

We know the body needs exercise and we understand that the brain needs regular workouts too. This could be a great time to broaden your interests and find a new subject to study. Choosing an unfamiliar topic can challenge our thinking processes and encourage our creativity, helping us to perceive the world from a new perspective. Take a moment to think about a new subject to study and open your mind to new possibilities. Your brain will most certainly appreciate the workout in refreshingly unfamiliar territory. A more active mental faculty is a superb addition to the way we think, analyse and interpret data, a finely tuned and more acute apparatus for appraising critical facts and assessing information. It's surprising how often an answer or solution to a problem pops up in the middle of a completely unrelated activity. That's why it's so helpful to study new subjects. How about a new language?

79. Stand up and relieve the tension in your muscles and joints

If you spend more than twenty minutes sitting in the same position, your joints will begin to stiffen and you'll increase the probability of pain and discomfort in your back, hips, knees and shoulders. So stand up and move around every twenty to thirty minutes and unlock your posture. Breathe a little more deeply and you'll refresh your brain too. Movement and breathing. We evolved to be active so sitting for hours at a time in front of a desk is one of the most unnatural things we can do. Get up and move. Our focus of attention can keep us locked to the computer screen for hours at a time. If you want to improve your efficiency, stand up every twenty minutes or so, stretch and breathe, move around a little and see how much more alert you feel when you go back to your work station. It sounds incredibly simple but it's a major way to boost your efficiency.

80. Sweet, white and deadly. The danger of sugar

Sugar provides us with an instant burst of energy but are you getting too much sugar in your diet, especially the highly refined sugars that are found in many processed foods? Cutting down on your total sugar intake can make a major difference to your health and help you to lose weight. That spike of energy you get from your sugar intake encourages your body to produce insulin which will flush excess glucose from your bloodstream, leading to a rapid decline in energy. So, instead of boosting your energy levels and powering you up to cut through the day's challenges, sugar leads to an inevitable decline in attention, focus and concentration. Cut down on sugar and help your body to maintain its natural, healthy balance as well as its optimum energy levels. We simply did not evolve to have so much processed sugar in our diet and it's poisoning our bodies. That's a fact. Cut down on sugars now before they have a chance to cut you down and degrade your quality of life. It's nothing more than a simple request for you to respect the miracle of your body. We want you to live long and enjoy a successful life with the best possible health. Sugar cannot be part of that picture.

81. The evil weed. Time to quit and place your vote for health and wellbeing

I grew up at a time when smoking was almost a universal pastime and everyone seemed to use tobacco. My parents smoked. My brothers smoked. It was considered absolutely normal. And I smoked too. But if there's one thing that improves your health and life expectancy, it must be giving up smoking. Despite our knowledge that tobacco is harmful, we still see people of all ages smoking. Make sure you limit your exposure to passive smoking too. If you or your friends or family still smoke, take a stand today and encourage everyone to give it up. Encourage your loved ones to quit. Because if you truly care about yourself and the people around you, be the inspiration in their lives to live a much healthier life. You cannot smoke and enjoy health self-esteem. You don't poison what you love. We've known about the dangers of tobacco for decades, especially the chemically-cured leaves that are used in cigarettes. How we can continue to poison ourselves with cigarettes in the face of overwhelming evidence and constant public health campaigns is a mystery. Quit right now.

82. Go natural. Choose the best fuel for your mind and for your body

Nutrition is such an important subject for all us because it represents the fuel that powers everything we do in our lives. But many of us are aware that processed food might not be the healthiest option for complete well-being. Nutritionists advise us to limit our intake of processed foods and try to ensure that seventy five percent of what we eat is unprocessed. My concern is that you might only begin to notice the harmful effects of processed foods as you get older. The time to adjust your dietary habits is now. Make a decision right this minute to boost your daily intake of natural, unprocessed food and take notice of the difference it makes to your energy levels, how your skin texture improves, how much better you sleep and how much easier it is to stay healthy. You might notice improvements in brain function too and this is another important benefit of smart nutrition. If we are what we eat, let's make a commitment to fuelling the body with the most natural and healthy food we can find. It's your body. It's the only one you've got. It's time to take good care of it. It's part of the package for totally successful living.

FREE GIFT FOR YOU OUR READER

…..enjoy this free ebook and more!

http://www.skinnydeliciouslife.com/free-epigenetic-diet-ebook

83. Grin and learn to enjoy your success every day

Smiling is good for you. Research suggests that smiling can even stimulate the brain and prolong the efficiency of our mental faculties. So amongst all the exercises that we use to stay in good physical shape, we need to remember the importance of stimulating our brains. Keep those brain cells active. We also need to appreciate any progress or success that we achieve along the way. Take stock of every day. Review your To Do list and assess how you spent your time. Did you use the day well and complete all your tasks? Did anything get in the way? Learn from every single day. This will help you to refine your activities and keep you firmly on track towards your goals. It takes work. But remember to smile!

Your mind needs mental press ups and weight training to keep it in peak condition in the same way that your body needs exercise to maintain health and well-being. And now we realise that the simple act of smiling can help to maintain our minds in a healthier and stronger condition. Besides, don't you feel better when you laugh? Don't you look younger when you smile? Don't you feel more confident with a happy grin on your face? Let laughter take its place in your daily routines and see what a positive difference it can make to your life.

84. Are you happy with your own company?

Are you able to spend time alone and feel absolutely fine? It's wonderful to enjoy the company of family and friends but it's very important that we learn to feel at ease with ourselves. I often refer to the destructive habit in our culture of judging everyone, including ourselves. But if we really want to create a lasting and deeply seated sense of personal happiness and well-being, we need to be comfortable and at ease with ourselves. Ultimately, this new-found level of self-acceptance can help us to feel more comfortable with the success that we achieve. We tend to feel more deserving of the good things we're bringing into our lives. We do not have to be perfect. We certainly don't need to pretend to be perfect. But we do need to accept ourselves.
It's liberating to acknowledge our mistakes and weaknesses but not helpful to dwell on them. When we feel at peace with ourselves, it is so much easier to be at peace with others. It doesn't mean we have to pretend to like everyone nor expect everyone to like us. This is irrelevant. Just be at peace with yourself and see how this peace is more easily reflected in the people around you and in the speed of your progress towards your brightly successful vision of the future.

85. Suspend all critical and destructive judgement of your body

Let's stop judging our bodies. Right now. It's distracting and takes away too much energy from the important issues on your personal Hit List. People see themselves in the mirror and make the most extraordinary judgements, usually negative and often quite insulting. And these judgements are harmful. Why do we react to our bodies in this way? Are we constantly comparing our bodies to the images displayed on television, in magazines, in the make-believe world of advertising?

These unfair judgements on our bodies only reflect our inner insecurities and have little to do with reality. It's time to make peace with our bodies. It's time to learn to appreciate the miracle that our bodies represent. So when you get out of bed in the morning and shuffle to the bathroom, please smile at yourself in the mirror. You might feel slightly absurd or even self-conscious but that doesn't matter. Smile at yourself and begin to change your relationship with your body.

If you want your body to be fitter, healthier, stronger and powered up with more energy and bounce, start by showing your appreciation for what your body gives you. It'll be the start of a beautiful new relationship. When you focus on your body by appreciating its positive aspects, you'll feel more inclined to look after it with a kinder, more supportive attitude and that's a fantastically effective way to boost your health and start to take better care of yourself. Because you deserve it.

86. Take a load off your feet and off your stomach

Do you ever stand while you're eating? Some cultures consider this behaviour to be harmful for the digestion. It is always better to be seated when you eat, to help your digestive system, to relax and put your body into a calmer state of being. Enjoying food is one is life's great pleasures but helping your body to process the food efficiently can improve digestion dramatically. So, whenever possible, sit down to eat, slow down, relax and enjoy the experience. And breathe. Mindfulness training encourages us to be more aware of what we're doing and this applies equally to eating. We learn to appreciate the taste and texture of our food. We slow down and allow the digestive system to function normally, burning the food as fuel rather than storing it as fat. You notice when you've eaten enough so you avoid the habit of over-eating. You create a precious oasis of calm in the day to allow yourself the luxury of relaxation and contemplation. It's another of those moments when your creativity processes the day's data and suggests better ways of resolving the challenges. Eating slowly, seated, relaxed and breathing gently. Try it today. Make it a habit. Make a note of how different you feel.

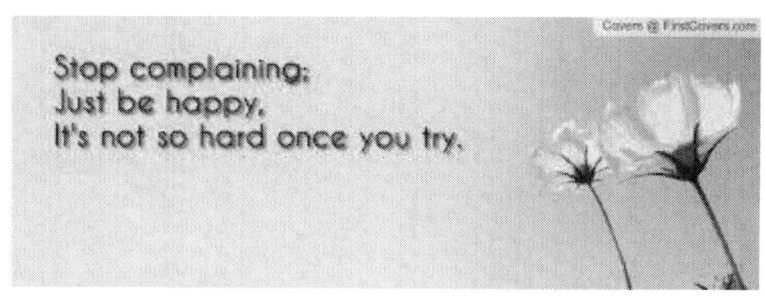

87. Whining and demeaning

Time to stop complaining. We spend far too much time and energy complaining about the state of the world, our lives, the universe in general and right now is simply the perfect moment to give up this negative and counter-productive habit of complaining. You probably know that whatever you focus on tends to become the dominant issue in your life. When you focus on complaining rather than improving the situation, you're telling yourself that things can't be better, that you don't have the power or the creativity to make a difference. Stop complaining about the problems and challenges. Start right now to focus on how you want things to be. Engage your creativity. Take action. Do something. Make a difference. Complaining is easy. But don't devalue your dreams, your abilities and your potential by wringing your hands and pretending your life has to be the way it is. Choose something better. Choose something that inspires or motivates you. Turn the old habit of complaining into the new habit of being positively engaged with the world. That's a difference that will work for you and everybody around you. It has been extremely rare in my experience to encounter super successful people who complained. When something was wrong or below standard, they took action. Immediately. Successful individuals don't whine.

88. Posture Checking. Attitude adjusting.

Are you doing this regularly? Are you sitting comfortably?? Good. Then let's begin. There's a high probability that you sit in the same position for far too long during the day. Not just the same position. Probably the wrong position too! Vast numbers of people spend their day hunched in front of a computer screen, hammering away at a keyboard, hardly breathing, moving a mouse round a mouse pad and wondering why their bodies get uncomfortable, stiff and tired. This rigid conformity to a fixed position is clearly uncomfortable for the body but it also traps us into one mode of thinking. When you adjust your physical position, you can make changes to your mental appreciation of the situation too. Meetings are another potential source of discomfort. The fact is that humans rarely sustain their focus and attention for more than twenty minutes at a time so those hours-long meetings can sap the will and energy of all the participants. The answer to this particular pair of problems is incredibly easy and simple. All you have to do is move. We referred to this before but it's so important, I'm repeating the message. Get up and move. Stretch. Breathe. Every twenty minutes. It's a fabulous way to boost your concentration and productivity.

89. Adequate Vitamin D. Get some rays!

Are you getting enough sunshine? Despite all the scare stories about the effects of sunlight on our skin, most Northern Europeans are surprisingly deficient in Vitamin D. The effects of too little exposure to the sun can be surprising. Even in the Summer, we cover up and apply total block sun screens, hide under beach umbrellas and avoid getting the sun on our skin. Too much exposure can obviously cause damage to the skin but too little is often a source of different kinds of health problems. Vitamin D deficiency can produce problems in the immune system, mental and emotional imbalance and interfere with the body's metabolic function, leading to depleted energy levels and muscle fatigue. Supplements are one solution but the body prefers to produce Vitamin D naturally from moderate exposure to sunlight. And sunbathing is a much more fun way to boost your body's health. If you can't get sunshine, consider the benefits of daily supplements. Vitamin D has been identified as one of the vital ingredients in regulating body weight so don't let your levels fall below body's minimum requirements. I'm writing these guidelines on the sunlit terrace of my home overlooking the Mediterranean, gentle waves lapping against the shoreline and seabirds following the fishing boats as they bring in the morning catch. This is how I get my daily dose of Vitamin D and it feels really, really good!

90. Amore and the building blocks of the Universe

Love is a dominant concept in our culture, promoted by stories, film, drama and popular myth. Perhaps the word fails to convey the deeper power that lies concealed within its more superficial aspects. Perhaps the better word would be 'acceptance' because this implies a lesser role for the ego and a more complete expression of how to be at peace with ourselves and the world around us. Acceptance does not require us to accept inappropriate behaviour. It doesn't blind us to the qualities we may see in ourselves and in others. But it allows us to experience a more direct connection to our deeper selves and the true potential that lies within everyone else. As a culture, we may well be in love with love but the pathway to peace and understanding is paved with a deeper capacity to accept ourselves and the people around us. These are certainly not new ideas but, in an age of superficiality, it is reassuring to recognise that we are capable of extremely powerful expressions of selfless love. Successful living means that we can enjoy deep and fulfilling relationships with ourselves and with others. It's part of the total richness of life. This beautiful concept of profound acceptance is the cornerstone of experiencing life as a constantly evolving miracle and our lives are deeply enriched by its wonderful generosity.

91. Data overload and the space within ourselves.

We live in a world that is flooded with information, images, distractions and stress. Do you ever take the time to switch off your mind and give it a well-deserved rest? One of the most effective ways to train the mind to become still is to meditate. The practise is so helpful to our health and wellbeing that it should form an integral part of our daily routines. Ideally we should meditate when we wake and before we go to bed, learning to bring the mind to a place of natural calm and stillness. Simply relax and breathe gently and learn to ignore the constant chatter of your mind until it gradually gives up the lifelong habit of constant activity and becomes still. In the Vedic tradition, this is a treasured place of great wisdom and insight, of calm and power, of understanding and balance. If these precious gifts can be found in the silence of meditation, let us begin today and reap the rewards that can only be found in the timeless space of inner silence.

92. The eternal power of the present moment

Time dominates our lives from the moment the alarm clock wakes us to the last moment of the day before we go to sleep. Our lives have undoubtedly become more organised, regulated by the unforgiving discipline of the clock. But time is supposed to serve us rather than control our every action. The pressure of the daily schedule can create enormous stress on our minds and bodies and shift our perspective into a constant contest between looking over our shoulders at the past and imagining the oncoming future. The problem is that we never really occupy this moment of power that is the present moment. Everything that we intend to do, think, feel or experience is rooted in this present moment. The past has gone. We need to let go of the past. The future has not been written. All is created and decided in the present. Becoming calm and experiencing the power of the present allows us to focus clearly on whatever future we desire. If we simply repeat the same thoughts, feelings and actions, we will always have the same results. If we change how we think and feel, we will create a different and perhaps better future, simply by making full use of this sacred, magical moment of the present.

93. Being real. Being who you are

Do you ever feel pressured to be nice to people that you simply don't like? I'm not encouraging anyone to be hostile or to harbour negative feelings about themselves or others but it is important to recognise that we do not have to like everybody. It's an extra layer of pressure that forces us to behave in ways that are completely unauthentic. One of my mentors suggested that when you reach that kind of understanding and accept that there's no room for progress, you have to move on. Acknowledging to yourself that you don't like someone can encourage us to understand why we don't like that particular individual. Too often the problem is that they remind us at some deep, uncomfortable level of ourselves! Understanding why we don't like certain individuals can help us move beyond the habit of judgement and learn to be around people without feeling defensive, hostile or uncomfortable. Ultimately, if we learn to be comfortable with ourselves, it is much easier to be comfortable around everyone else. Then you don't have to pretend at all. One of the biggest obstacles to total success is a deeply held conviction that we don't deserve to have all the good things that would life so much better. Many people often counter their achievements with negative behaviour, as if the success of their hard work has to be paid for in some bizarrely destructive way. We make some money, so we wreck our health. We create a successful business but neglect our loved ones. We control our financial empire and turn to drugs or alcohol to handle the pressure. I've seen it so often. Yet it absolutely does not have to be like this. That's why we're committed to total success. My mentors warned me of the dangers of not feeling worthy. They believed wholeheartedly in the potential for total success in every area of life. I got the message. And I'm passing on the torch of good news and prosperity to you.

94. Harnessing the power of change.

Your personal Hit List is a call for change. Your goals and dreams and ambitions demand action. And that means something has to be different. For thousands of years we have understood that our lives are deeply influenced by our thoughts and feelings. Humans are incredibly creative but too often we use our mental and emotional energy to focus on wholly negative outcomes. It's part of our evolution. We learned to anticipate danger to ensure our survival. But when we focus entirely on the problems and difficulties, that's all we see. How much more powerful to focus on the positive, desired outcomes that make life so much better. Concentrate on your goals and dreams and how to make them a reality. How different the world appears when we engage positive thoughts and feelings. The great challenge is to be aware of this potential for creativity and channel it towards positive results. Begin today and see how quickly things can improve. The potential for positive change applies to every single aspect of our lives. Total success means engaging our creativity and applying it to every area of our lives. This creates opportunities for change and improvement every single day. Life is so precious. Let us not waste any part of it.

95. Emotional energy and the powerhouse that drives the Universe

Where does the energy for change come from? How is it possible to harness our energy and direct it towards a brighter, healthier future? The answer is in our emotions. Our emotional energy drives the greater part of our lives. Our pre-conditioned feelings and emotional responses determine much of what happens in our lives and how we deal with it. But our emotional energy is so powerful that the moment we learn to direct it towards any outcome that we desire, our lives immediately begin to move in this new direction. Our emotional framework provides the outline for our lives. Our emotions are the compass of our life's direction. You don't have to believe this but, if you're willing to experiment with the concept, you will soon realise how much influence you can extend over your life and circumstances. Life doesn't just happen. We are deeply connected to the way our lives unfold. We influence every aspect of the events that touch our existence. Let's accept this powerful force for change as a positive gift that can put our lives onto the best possible track for complete, all round wellbeing and a whole new concept of the meaning of success.

96. Recognising the power and value of our dreams

There are countless stories of successful individuals receiving powerful insights into their business situations through the medium of their dreams. Do you remember your dreams? There's evidence that everyone dreams but we're not always aware of the experience. However, as I've mentioned before, dreams can provide powerful insights into the state of our life and give very precise clues into our current state of development and, perhaps, where we need to focus our conscious attention. The content of our dreams is often purely symbolic. Literal interpretations are rarely reliable. We need to write down our dreams as soon as we wake, enlisting the co-operation of our subconscious to hold and recall the images and feelings. The details can provide a rich source of material and, once we learn to decode the symbolism, we can have access to an extraordinary range of profound observations, answers to problems and questions, insights into our nature as well as gaining extraordinary analysis of what we can do to enhance our chances to be successful. All from the simple experience of our dreams. Start tonight. Tell yourself that you'll remember your dreams when you wake and have a pen and paper handy to jot down whatever you can recall. Welcome to the wonderful world of your own subconscious.

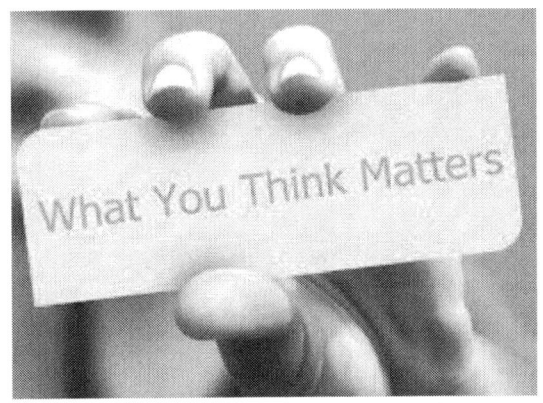

97. You are what you think.

How often have you heard that expression? It's a concept that can shape your entire future. Henry Ford was often quoted as saying "Whether you think you can or whether you think you can't – you're right." As you learn to break free from the limitations of your background, you can shape powerful, positive new thoughts and images that will lead to a more fulfilling life. These ideas are not new. They've been part of the human experience for thousands of years and, thanks to modern communications, have never been easier to access. Our health, our success, our relationships, our purpose in this world can all be enhanced by consciously focusing on positive thoughts and feelings. Developing simple affirmations can offset all the baggage and restrictions of the past. Find positive expressions to describe how you want your life to be. Repeat your affirmations as often as you can. Print them out and put them where you can see them all the time. Engage your new vision and see your life evolve along its new, happier, healthier pathway. Positive expressions will produce an emotional response. That raw emotional fuel can produce subtle shifts in your neural pathways, allowing for a more creative, expansive view of your circumstances. Suddenly you feel more confident, empowered, free to take on the next set of challenges, ready to experience the thrill of hitting your targets and realising your dreams.

98. Once you accept the power of choice in your life, everything begins to move forwards

In the course of advising corporate entities and their senior management, I've sometimes heard people describe their reactions, attitudes and behaviours as inevitable, that in some way their personalities and viewpoints are no more than a product of their backgrounds or upbringing or even a result of their DNA. Sometimes we excuse our attitudes by blaming our parents for being the way we are. But this cannot be so. We possess a powerful tool for change in our species and that is our ability to choose. We can choose what we do, we can choose what we think, we can even choose how we feel. The real issue is to determine if the way you are right now truly represents how you want to be. Let's stop blaming others for how we are. Let's exercise choice. This is the perfect moment for you let go of habits and behaviours that degrade your capacity for complete fulfilment and self-expression. It's time to practise the art of becoming who we really are. This is a pathway to freedom and success for ourselves and for those with whom we are most closely connected. This is how life becomes so much more enjoyable.

99. Reviewing progress and taking the next step.

It's time to consult your Hit List, your personal collection of items that you felt were missing from your life. Write down everything you've done so far to address the most important issues. Has the list changed? Have you added or deleted any items? Is the list evolving along with your changing perspective? Do you now have a real wish list? A list of the things that you really want to have in your life? This list can be very helpful in assisting you to identify not only what you feel might be missing from your life but, perhaps more importantly, why you felt the need for certain things in the first place. The list is still private. It's not for sharing or discussion. It's your list. Usually, after you've identified the most obvious material improvements in your life, you start to think about some of the emotional areas that might need some work. But it's very helpful to ask yourself why you've chosen the particular items that take up the first dozen or so places on your list. This analysis can shed light on why you think you do things. This is where the list becomes really useful. As you return to your list - perhaps once a week will be enough - you might notice that some of the items are no longer important to you. Your priorities are changing. New areas emerge. Most lists take time to mature and evolve. This is when the list can become your focal point for further action, giving shape and form to your goals, dreams and deepest wishes. This where a more complete vision of total success emerges.

100. Drink deeply from the wellspring of your deeper mind.

Do you ever take time to find a calmer, more relaxed state of mind during the day? Meditation is a vital tool for training the mind and body to relax but, if you feel you don't have time during the day to meditate, you might try a mini-meditation that only takes a few minutes. I first came across the technique in India but was pleasantly surprised many years later when one of my mentors suggested the same method as a way of re-focusing the mind. It's simply a matter of sitting quietly, breathing more deeply and more slowly, relaxing your neck, back and shoulders and bringing your attention to a fixed point. Perhaps a simple picture or image can act as a focal point, allowing you to concentrate on the present moment, releasing the stresses and tensions of the day, bringing your awareness to a deeper state of calm, renewing your energy and stabilising your emotions. Practising this simple technique only requires a minute or two but it is so easy to incorporate into your daily routine that you can use it every hour of the day to regain your natural balance and equilibrium. The benefits filter into every aspect of your life. As you relax from the reflexive attitudes of stress and tension, your perspective changes and you re-engage your creativity. The subconscious whispers gently and offers profound insights into your situation. Your deeper mind lends its weight to your efforts. Your confidence emerges from the shadows of stress and you know you can take care of everything.

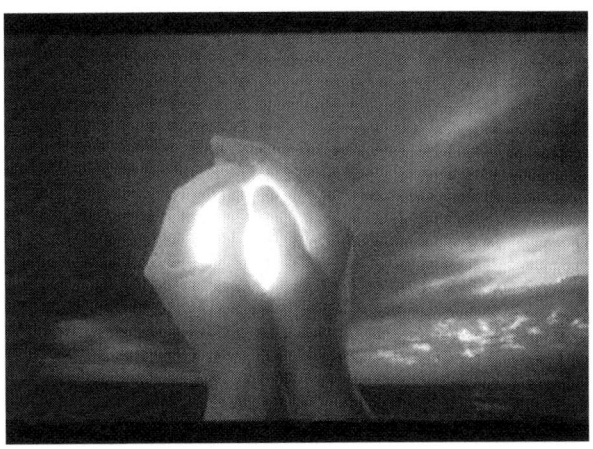

101. The imagination. Visualising the brightest possible future

Many hyper successful individuals could be described as visionaries but they could all imagine clearly where they wanted to be. The imagination is an extraordinary key to accessing the driving power and influence of our subconscious. It's important to remember that much of our behaviour is rooted in our subconscious programming, driving our thoughts and emotional expression, driving our actions and even affecting our choice of partner. But are we condemned to follow this programming for the whole of our lives or can we change it? The good news is that we can make remarkable changes to this programming and produce equally remarkable changes in our lives. Our imagination is full of symbolism and this is the dominant language of the subconscious. By learning to direct our imagination and focus on appropriate symbols, we can begin to cancel inappropriate beliefs and ways of thinking and replace them with positive, affirming attitudes that enhance the quality of our lives at every level. A fulfilled and fulfilling life can be founded on these simple yet powerful principles. So what kind of symbols could we use? Once you know what you want to create in your life, find pictures that most closely represent your goals and ambitions. Place the pictures around your home, around your workplace, so that you're constantly reminded of what it would feel like to experience whatever's in your illustrations. You can choose whatever you want. It's your life. But choose things that excite you. Choose things that speak to you at the deepest possible level. You're mapping out your life. Make it truly magnificent. Make it totally successful.

About the Author

Initially I trained in the field of Corporate Psychology and Management, gaining a PhD along the way and spending most of my time driving commercial projects and delivering Motivational Training in a corporate environment.And there were catalysts for change that appeared quite unexpectedly. I've been privileged to sit at the feet of some quite extraordinary financial giants, individuals who carved out their success from the bare rock of their own determination and dogged persistence. These were highly motivated and inspiring people and it's largely thanks to their advice and unwavering examples that I've been able to create a lifestyle that allows me to enjoy the kind of freedom that most people only dream about.

MY INSPIRATION

I have been extremely fortunate to work with a surprising number of self-made billionaires, individuals who were generous enough to share their experiences and their personal philosophy of success with me. Some of them were kind enough to mentor me during my earlier years and this generosity has prompted me to publish and share some of the jewels of their accumulated wisdom and add weight to the argument that success is not an accident.

As well as studying the architecture of material success, these individuals also dwelt on the importance of creating balance in life, of creating time to be with their families, to support great causes and to make a difference to the quality of peoples' lives. They appreciated the freedom that their lifestyles had created for themselves and displayed a breath-taking lack of selfishness in promoting success wherever they found fertile ground in which their advice could take root. One of them described this spirit of generosity as a personal legacy, a way of ensuring that all of his hard-won lessons were not simply confined to the limits of his own life.

There's a great deal of material in the marketplace today on the subject of success. Against this dense background of conflicting ideas and approaches, perhaps we should determine from the outset what success really entails.

I subscribe to my mentors' philosophy of personal freedom, of creating sufficient wealth to live the way you want to live and to enjoy the gift of this life to the full. You'll feel a lot better when you share your success with others too. You certainly don't have to be a billionaire to achieve that level of freedom and personal choice or to make a difference to the lives of others. But you do need the appropriate attitude. You will need determination and you'll probably need to make some adjustments to how you think, feel and behave. Letting go of old habits, shaking yourself loose from the grip of the past, learning to focus on a much brighter vision of the future – these are all components that will enhance your chances for success and improve the quality of your daily life at every level. It isn't simply a question of how much cash you've stashed away. The picture's bigger, more detailed, more encompassing and brighter than you might've thought possible. Success is certainly about measurable achievement but it also involves a stronger connections to the people around us. It involves a deep sense of peace within ourselves. It encapsulates the concept of personal acceptance. It permits us to choose appropriate goals and to follow the winding pathway to our destination with unbreakable confidence in our ability to get wherever we choose to go. And, if the seeds of wisdom have taken root, to enjoy the journey to the full.

Other Bestselling Books by the Author

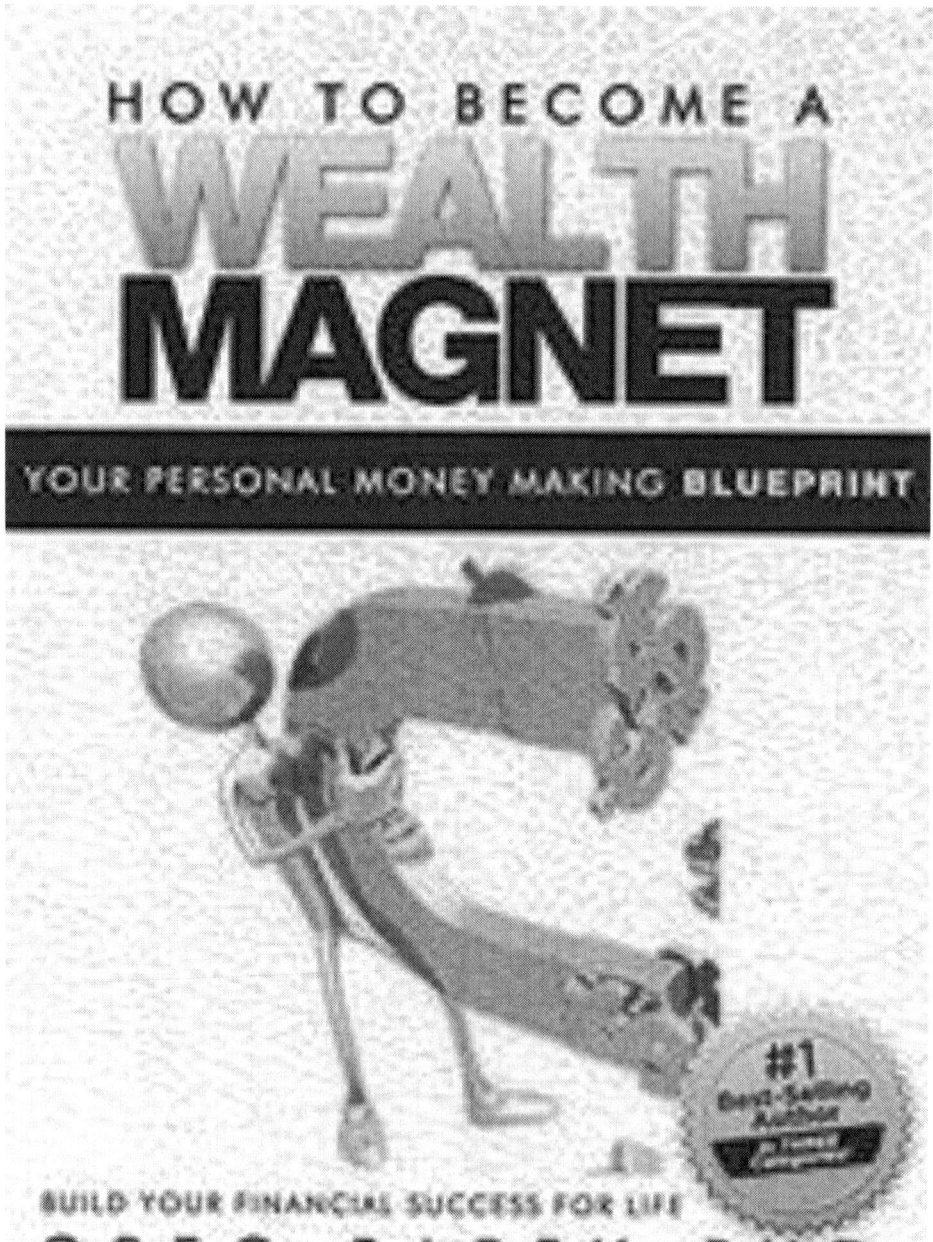

Printed in Great Britain
by Amazon